How to Use the Power of the Printed Word

How to Use the Power of the Printed Word

Thirteen articles packed with facts and practical information, designed to help you read better, write better, communicate better.

Malcolm Forbes   Erma Bombeck
Bill Cosby   Tony Randall
Kurt Vonnegut   Edward T. Thompson
Steve Allen   James A. Michener
George Plimpton   Jane Bryant Quinn
James Dickey   John Irving
              Russell Baker

PREFACE BY

Clifton Fadiman

EDITED BY

Billings S. Fuess, Jr.

ANCHOR PRESS
DOUBLEDAY & COMPANY, INC., GARDEN CITY, NEW YORK
1985

Grateful acknowledgment is made to the following for use of their photographs of the contributors:

Malcolm Forbes, Copyright © by Bob Forbes; Tony Randall, Copyright © by John Cahoon; Bill Cosby, Edward T. Thompson, Kurt Vonnegut, James A. Michener, and Russell Baker, Copyright © by Harold Krieger; Steve Allen and Erma Bombeck, Copyright © by Marc Feldman; Jane Bryant Quinn and George Plimpton, Copyright © by Michael Pateman; James Dickey, Copyright © 1982 by Mark Morrow; John Irving, Copyright © by Steve Steigman.

Grateful acknowledgment is made to the following for use of their illustrations: p. 28, Copyright © by Arnold Levin; p. 42, Copyright © by Little Apple Art.

Library of Congress Cataloging in Publication Data
Main entry under title:
How to Use the Power of the printed word.
    "Articles have appeared . . . in magazine and newspaper advertisements sponsored by International Paper Company"—T.p. verso.
    Bibliography: p. 108.
    1. English language—Study and teaching—United States —Addresses, essays, lectures.   2. Language arts—United States—Addresses, essays, lectures.   3. Communication— United States—Addresses, essays, lectures.   4. Youth— United States—Books and reading—Addresses, essays, lectures.   I. Forbes, Malcolm S.   II. Fuess, Billings S. III. International Paper Company.
LB1576.H674   1985   428'.007   82-45195
ISBN 0-385-18215-5
ISBN 0-385-18216-3 (pbk.)

Contents

Preface

Let me tell you about a man I know.

When he started out in life, he didn't seem to have much going for him. His parents spoke imperfect English. Being poor, they couldn't give him any "advantages." Most of his schoolmates were like himself—slum kids or not much better. Though healthy enough, he grew up shortish and no great shakes as an athlete. His mother may have liked his face, but it would never win a beauty prize. Worst of all, he turned out to have no head for business.

In only one way was he above the average. He liked words. He liked their shape, their sound and the way they fitted together to make clear or surprising or useful statements. He liked to read, write, speak and listen to them.

Because he had few other talents, he concentrated on his ability to handle words. As the years rolled by, he was astonished to find that he was making for himself a reasonably interesting, respectable and successful life. And he was accomplishing this almost entirely through his capacity to speak, write, read and listen a little better than most others.

He's an old man now. But not a day passes that he does not bless the English language and offer up a prayer for its health and welfare.

That old man—sure, you guessed it—is the writer of these lines. Because I owe so much to the power of the printed and spoken word, I've tried to pay back a little of my debt by persuading young people that that power really exists. It can help to make your life more interesting. But more to the point, if you

have no command at all over that power, you'll be sadly handi-
capped no matter what you go in for. Unless you're a rock star.

Because I feel this so deeply, I'm glad to add my small bit to
International Paper's crusade to help young Americans read,
write and speak better. It's interesting that one of our great
industrial concerns should back this campaign. What it shows is
that thoughtful businessmen are worried over the decline in our
capacity to talk to each other, write to each other, and learn from
the printed word whatever it can tell us about our lives. Success
in business, of course, depends on many factors. But the people
who run great American enterprises like International Paper
know that one *big* factor is the ability to handle words clearly,
honestly, persuasively.

And so they sponsored a series of advertisements—they're
really little essays—written by successful Americans. These advertisements are now collected in this small book. Read it carefully. Try to act on some of the advice given. In school or out of
it, you can't fail to benefit.

The people who here stand up to bear witness to the power
and magic of the word vary in talent. Some are distinguished
professional writers, a few are journalists, one is an entertainer-
educator, another a television star who doubles as a versatile
actor, one an actor, one an editor, and one is a highly successful
businessman. They talk about different things: business letters,
vocabulary, libraries, the classics, poetry, speechmaking, speed-
reading, spelling, punctuation. But really, they're all talking
about the same thing: communication.

The communication may be practical: writing a business
letter in accordance with the sensible rules laid down by Malcolm Forbes. Or it may take the higher form discussed by Steve
Allen: communicating with Huckleberry Finn or Hamlet. Whatever the communication experience may be, if it's engaged in
seriously, you emerge from it with a deeper knowledge of yourself. We grow by connecting with each other. A hermit isn't very
interesting. Or, to put it another way, it takes a great communi-

cator to *make* him interesting, as Defoe did with Robinson Crusoe.

These thirteen talks about reading and writing cover a lot of ground, quickly and clearly. I'd like to add two more thoughts. The first has to do with the usefulness of *listening*. We do listen to TV and radio, but a great deal of it isn't worth the time spent on it. We might gain more by listening, with respect and attention, to each other, to our teachers, our family and to those few voices on the air that really have something to say and know how to say it. The basic listening rule is simple: Keep your mind not on yourself but on the other fellow.

The second matter I'd like to stress has to do with reading. Get in the habit of reading above what you think is your proper level. High jumpers make records by hiking the bar a little at a time. It's the same with books or magazines. If you stick only with what you easily understand, your understanding won't grow. We don't deepen our reading enjoyment by immediately comprehending every word, sentence, paragraph and reference. We deepen it by grappling with the partly understood, the unfamiliar, the phrase or idea that forces us to think. Of course, I'm talking about reading above a certain level: The sign reading EXIT IN CASE OF FIRE is made up of words meant to be understood at once by all.

If you've gotten this far, I want to make a final plea for literacy. Let's put the plea in terms that should interest every one of us. I'm talking about survival. I don't mean merely physical survival. You might be able, as savages do, to live without being able to read Mr. Michener or Mr. Vonnegut. I'm talking about survival as civilized men and women, as citizens of a great country, as members of a human race that holds itself superior to the other animals.

The fact is that the ability to read, write, talk and understand has in our time become a survival tool, just as the flint ax was a survival tool for our ancestors. That ability is not only a *sign* of intelligence. It also *develops* the intelligence. Without it we're only second-class citizens, half slaves, surely not free men and women. We don't have to become highbrows or intellectuals to remain free. But we do have to be able to communicate with each other, learn from each other, judge our leaders and our laws. Democracy and literacy go together.

Let me clinch the point with four sentences. I wish you'd memorize them. They were written years ago by a great philosopher, Alfred North Whitehead. But they're truer than ever. Paste them on your mirror.

In the conditions of modern life the rule is absolute, the race which does not value trained intelligence is doomed.

Not all your heroism, not all your social charm, not all your wit, not all your victories on land or at sea, can move back the finger of fate.

To-day we maintain ourselves.

Tomorrow science will have moved forward yet one more step, and there will be no appeal from the judgement which will then be pronounced on the uneducated.

Clifton Fadiman

Introduction

The essays in this collection are the fruits of our efforts so far to try to help all Americans, especially *young* Americans, learn the value of—and learn to make better use of—*the power of the printed word.*

We started the series in 1979 as a corporate advertising campaign for International Paper Company. The essays appear in magazines and newspapers geared to reach young people. You may have seen some of them.

The whole thing came about when International Paper asked us at Ogilvy & Mather, their advertising agency, how they could help publishers of books, magazines and newspapers understand that IP is not just another disinterested supplier of paper, but an active, caring partner in their businesses and concerns.

We all agreed that the best way to show IP's commitment to publishers would be to help the printed word attract a healthy future audience, the lifeblood of any publisher.

And we knew exactly how to go about it.

Encourage young people to understand the value of the printed word—and become more comfortable with and more skillful at the use of it. So this series, *How to Use the Power of the Printed Word,* was born.

The fact is, the decline in America's ability to read and write, the lack of effective use of the printed word, should concern us all—as parents, who may see trouble signs in our own children's reading and writing abilities; as business people, who must cope daily with a growing flow of written communications peppered with mistakes and fuzzy wording; and as thoughtful citizens who wonder whether democracy as we now know it can survive if our people can't make good use of the printed word. Our forefathers based our democracy from the beginning on the consent of a people who can read and write and express themselves.

Our aim was to tell young people not just *why they should,* but *how to* read and write better. So our authors and I, as editor, went about doing just that—and jam-packed as much information into each article as we possibly could. We've never shifted our sights.

I think we've succeeded in our intent. One college professor told me that he was surprised to find that Malcolm Forbes's article on "How to write a business letter" contained as much useful information as the *seven* books that he uses for each business class.

As for contributors, we carefully chose those whose credentials would instantly ring true to young people and whose character and styles of expression would appeal to that audience, whether the authors were familiar to them or not.

I think we've succeeded again. We were lucky enough to get the participation of the outstanding writers collected here for you. They all believed in our project so much that they managed to make time for it even though they were up to their eyeballs in important projects of their own.

Each one was, in his or her own special way, a delight to work with—extremely gifted and at the same time disciplined and thoroughly professional. What's more, the writers of these essays are good company and fun to be with.

I vividly remember cracking Chesapeake Bay blue crab with James A. Michener and his wife Mari at the harbor in St. Michaels, Maryland. And getting personal instruction from James Dickey on how to shoot a primitive blowgun in his lakeside backyard in Columbia, South Carolina. And laughing with Erma

Bombeck and then Russell Baker, both of whom just can't help saying tellingly funny things even in ordinary conversation.

I got great pleasure peeking at some of the titles of the thousands of books overflowing Steve Allen's office and home. Even as we worked, carpenters were frantically putting in *more* bookshelves up on the second floor of his house. And I went to great lengths—and enjoyed it—as I rode my cycle from the hills of New Jersey to Southampton, Long Island, to meet with John Irving, and then compared cycle-riding exploits with him.

Is our effort to help our fellow Americans read and write better doing any good? We think so, if even in a small way. Some evidence: Teachers report that the series, when they use it with accompanying guides prepared by *Scholastic* magazine, give a lively boost to classroom morale and to their students' interest in improving their skills with the printed word.

Another indication: International Paper Company receives an average of a thousand letters a day thanking the authors and the company for the articles and requesting additional copies. To date (as of March 1985), International Paper has sent out over *22 million* reprints.

Readers have praised the articles. So has the communications industry. In 1983 our series won the Stephen E. Kelly Award from the Magazine Publishers Association for the best magazine advertising campaign of the year. It has won more than a dozen awards, and has been commended by educators, businessmen and government leaders, including President Ronald Reagan.

Among the reasons for the kind of excited and exciting reception our series has found are our contributors, who brought sharp focus and good reading to the basic principles and suggestions you'll find here.

The series of articles in this book—and the book itself—would not have grown to this size or even seen the light of day without the encouragement and support of a number of people at International Paper Company. I'm thinking especially of Robert F. Lauterborn, Director of Marketing Communication and Corporate Advertising, who was first to sense the importance and power of the series; William Dodenhoff, then Senior Vice President of Pulp and Paper, who committed the first financial support; and over time, Chairmen of the Board J. Stanford Smith, Dr. Edwin A. Gee and John A. Georges, each of whom quickly recognized the value of the program to America's young people and firmly supported it.

As you can see, *all* of us believe in the power of the printed word. If you hold this book in your hands, we know that you do, too.

More power to you.
Billings Fuess

Summit, New Jersey
March 1, 1985

How to Use the
Power of the
Printed Word

We asked Malcolm Forbes, president and editor in chief of *Forbes* magazine, to share some things he's learned about writing a good business letter. One rule: "Be crystal clear."

Money is a burden most people wld be willing to carry.

To Colette Thanks! Malcolm

How to Write a Business Letter

by Malcolm Forbes

A good business letter can get you a job interview.

Get you off the hook.

Or get you money.

It's totally asinine to blow your chances of getting whatever you want by writing a business letter that turns people off instead of turning them on.

The best place to learn to write is in school. If you're still there, pick your teachers' brains.

If not, big deal. I learned to ride a motorcycle at fifty and fly balloons at fifty-two. It's never too late to learn.

Over ten thousand business letters come across my desk every year. They seem to fall into three categories: stultifying if not stupid, mundane (most of them), and first-rate (rare). Here's the approach I've found that separates the winners from the losers (most of it's just good common sense); it starts before you write your letters.

Know What You Want

If you aren't sure what you want in detail, write down what you're sure of in one sentence. "I want to get an interview within the next two weeks." That simple. List the major points you want to get across; it'll keep you on course.

If you're answering a letter, check the points that need answering and keep the letter in front of you while you write. This way you won't forget anything; that would cause another round of letters.

And for goodness' sake, answer promptly if you're going to answer at all. Don't sit on a letter; that invites the person on the other end to sit on whatever you want from him.

Plunge Right In

Call him by name—not "Dear Sir, Madam, or Ms." but "Dear Mr. Chrisanthopoulos"—and be sure to spell it right. That'll get him (thus you) off to a good start.

(Usually, you can get his name just by phoning his company, or from a business directory in your nearest library.)

Tell what your letter is about in the first paragraph. One or two sentences. Don't keep your reader guessing, or he might file your letter away—even before he finishes it.

In the round file.

If you're answering a letter, refer to the date it was written. So the reader won't waste time hunting for it.

People who read business letters are as human as thee and me. Reading a letter shouldn't be a chore; reward the reader for the time he gives you.

Write So He'll Enjoy It

Write the entire letter from his point of view—what's in it for him? Beat him to the draw: surprise him by answering the questions and objections he might have.

"Be natural. Imagine him sitting in front of
you—what would you say to him?"

Be positive—he'll be more receptive to what you have to say.

Be nice. Contrary to the cliché, genuinely nice guys most
often finish first or very near it. I admit it's not easy when you've
got a gripe. To be agreeable while disagreeing—that's an art.

Be natural—write the way you talk. Imagine him sitting in front
of you. What would you say to him?

Business jargon too often is cold, stiff, unnatural.

Suppose I came up to you and said, "I acknowledge receipt
of your letter and I beg to thank you." You'd think, "Huh?
You're putting me on."

The acid test: Read your letter out loud when you're done.

3

You might get a shock, but you'll know for sure if it sounds natural.

Don't be cute or flippant. The reader won't take you seriously. This doesn't mean you've got to be dull. You prefer your letter to knock 'em dead rather than bore 'em to death.

Three points to remember:

Have a sense of humor. That's refreshing anywhere—a nice surprise in a business letter.

Be specific. If I tell you there's a new fuel that could save gasoline, you might not believe me. But suppose I tell you this:

"Gasohol"—10 percent alcohol, 90 percent gasoline— works as well as straight gasoline. Since you can make alcohol from grain or cornstalks, wood or wood waste, coal—even garbage—it's worth some real follow- through.

Now you've got something to sink your teeth into.

Lean more heavily on nouns and verbs, more lightly on adjectives. Use the active voice instead of the passive. Your writing will have more guts.

Which of these is stronger? Active voice: "I kicked out my money manager." Or, passive voice: "My money manager was kicked out by me." (By the way, neither is true. My son, Malcolm Jr., manages most Forbes money. He's a brilliant moneyman.)

Give It the Best You've Got

When you don't want something enough to make the effort, making an effort is a waste.

Make your letter look appetizing—or you'll strike out before you even get to bat. Type it—on good-quality 8½″ × 11″ statio- nery. Keep it neat. And use paragraphing that makes it easier to read.

Keep your letter short—to one page if possible. Keep your

"I learned to ride a motorcycle at fifty and fly balloons at fifty-
   two. It's never too late to learn anything."

paragraphs short. After all, who's going to benefit if your letter
is quick and easy to read?

   You.

   For emphasis, *underline* important words. And sometimes
indent sentences as well as paragraphs.

Like this. See how well it works? (But save it for something special.)

Make it perfect. No typos, no misspellings, no factual errors. If you're sloppy and let mistakes slip by, the person reading your letter will think you don't know better or don't care. Do you?

Be crystal clear. You won't get what you're after if your reader doesn't get the message.

Use good English. If you're still in school, take all the English and writing courses you can. The way you write and speak can really help—or hurt.

If you're not in school (or even if you are), get the little seventy-one-page gem by William Strunk and E. B. White, *The Elements of Style.* It's in paperback. It's fun to read and loaded with tips on good English and good writing.

Don't put on airs. Pretense invariably impresses only the pretender.

Don't exaggerate. Even once. Your reader will suspect everything else you write.

Distinguish opinions from facts. Your opinions may be the best in the world. But they're not gospel. You owe it to your reader to let him know which is which. He'll appreciate it and he'll admire you. The dumbest people I know are those who Know It All.

Be honest. It'll get you further in the long run. If you're not, you won't rest easy until you're found out. (Concerning the latter, I'm not speaking from experience.)

Edit ruthlessly. Somebody ~~has~~ said that words are ~~a lot~~ like inflated money—the more ~~of them that~~ you use, the less each one ~~of them~~ is worth. ~~Right on.~~ Go through your entire letter just as many times as it takes. ~~Search out and~~ annihilate all unnecessary words, ~~and~~ sentences—even ~~entire~~ paragraphs.

Sum It Up and Get Out

The last paragraph should tell the reader exactly what you want him to do or what you're going to do. Short and sweet. "May I

"Don't exaggerate. Even once. Your reader will suspect everything else you write."

have an appointment? Next Monday, the 16th, I'll call your secretary to see when it'll be most convenient for you."

Close with something simple, such as "Sincerely." And for heaven's sake, sign legibly. The biggest ego trip I know is a completely illegible signature.

Good luck.

I hope you get what you're after.

Sincerely,

We asked Tony Randall, who is on the American Heritage Dictionary Usage Panel and loves words almost as much as acting, to tell us how he has acquired his enormous vocabulary.

2

How to Improve Your Vocabulary

by *Tony Randall*

Words can make us laugh, cry, go to war, fall in love.

Rudyard Kipling called words the most powerful drug of mankind. If they are, I'm a hopeless addict, and I hope to get you hooked, too.

Whether you're still in school or you head up a corporation, the better command you have of words, the better chance you have of saying exactly what you mean, of understanding what others mean and of getting what you want in the world.

English is the richest language—with the largest vocabulary on earth. Over one million words.

You can express shades of meaning that aren't even *possible* in other languages. (For example, you can differentiate between "sky" and "heaven." The French, Italians and Spanish cannot.)

Yet the average adult has a vocabulary of only thirty thousand to sixty thousand words. Imagine what we're missing!

Here are five pointers that help me learn—and remember— whole *families* of words at a time. They may not *look* easy, and won't be at first, but if you stick with them, you'll find they *work*.

What's the first thing to do when you see a word you don't know?

1. Try to Guess the Meaning of the Word from the Way It's Used

You can often get at least *part* of a word's meaning just from how it's used in a sentence.

That's why it's so important to read as much as you can— different *kinds* of things: magazines, books, newspapers you don't normally read. The more you expose yourself to new words, the more words you'll pick up *just by seeing how they're used.*

For instance, say you run across the word "manacle":

"The manacles had been on John's wrists for thirty years. Only one person had a key: his wife."

You have a good *idea* of what "manacles" are, just from the context of the sentence.

But let's find out *exactly* what the word means and where it comes from. The only way to do this, and to build an extensive vocabulary *fast,* is to go to the dictionary. (How lucky that you *can;* Shakespeare *couldn't.* There *wasn't* an English dictionary in his day.)

So you go to the dictionary. (NOTE: Don't let dictionary abbreviations put you off. Up front you'll find what they mean. You'll also find a guide to pronunciation symbols there, as well as an abbreviated version on each page.)

2. Look It Up

Here's the definition for "manacle" in *The American Heritage Dictionary of the English Language.*

man·a·cle (măn′ə-kəl) *n.* Usually plural. **1.** A device for confining the hands, usually consisting of two metal rings that are fastened about the wrists and joined by a metal chain; a handcuff. **2.** Anything that confines or restrains. —*tr.v.* **manacled, -cling, -cles.** **1.** To restrain with manacles. **2.** To confine or restrain as if with manacles; shackle; fetter. [Middle English *manicle,* from Old French, from Latin *manicula,* little hand, handle, diminutive of *manus,* hand. See **man-²** in Appendix.*]

10

"Your main clue to remembering a word is its
root—its *origin*."

The first definition fits here: "a device for confining the
hands, usually consisting of two metal rings that are fastened
about the wrists and joined by a metal chain; a handcuff."

Well, that's what you *thought* it meant. But what's the idea
behind the word? What are its *roots?* To really understand a
word, you need to know.

Here's where the detective work—and the *fun*—begins.

3. Dig the Meaning Out by the Roots

The root is the basic part of the word—its heritage, its origin.
(Most roots in English come from Latin and Greek words at least

" 'Emancipate' has a Latin root. Learn it and
you'll know other words at a glance."

two thousand years old, which come from even earlier Indo-
European tongues.)

Learning the roots: (1) helps us *remember* words; (2) gives us
a deeper understanding of the words we *already* know; and (3)
allows us to pick up whole families of *new* words at a time. That's
why learning the root is *the most important part of going to the
dictionary.*

Notice that the root of "manacle" is *manus* (Latin), meaning
"hand."

Well, that makes sense. Now other words with this root,
man, start to make sense, too.

Take *man*ual—something done "by hand" (*man*ual labor) or
a "handbook." And *man*age—to "handle" something (as a *man*-
ager). When you e*man*cipate someone, you're taking him "from
the hands of" someone else.

When you *man*ufacture something, you "make it by hand" (in its original meaning).

And when you finish your first novel, your publisher will see your (originally "handwritten") *man*uscript.

Imagine! A whole new world of words opens up—just from one simple root.

The root gives the basic clue to the meaning of a word. But there's another important clue that runs a close second: the *prefix.*

4. Get the Powerful Prefixes Under Your Belt

A prefix is the part that's sometimes attached to the front of a word. Such as—well, "*pre*fix." There aren't many—less than a hundred major prefixes—and you'll learn them in no time at all just by becoming more aware of the meanings of words you already know. Here are a few. (Some of the vocabulary-building how-to books will give you the others.)

PREFIX		MEANING	EXAMPLES	
(Lat.)	*(Gk.)*			*(Literal sense)*
com, con	sym, syn	with, very,	conform	(form with)
co, col, cor	syl	together	sympathy	(feeling with)
in, im,	a, an	not,	innocent	(not wicked)
il, ir		without	amor-phous	(without form)
contra,	anti,	against,	contravene	(come against)
counter	ant	opposite	antidote	(give against)

Now see how the prefix (along with the context) helps you get the meaning of the italicized words:

"If you're going to be my witness, your story must <u>*corroborate*</u> my story." (The literal meaning of *corroborate* is "strength together.")

"First you told me one thing—now you tell me another. Don't <u>*contradict*</u> yourself." (The literal meaning of *contradict* is "say against.")

"The more words you know, the more you can use. What does 'corroborate' *really* mean? See the text."

"Oh, that snake's not poisonous. It's a completely <u>*innocuous*</u> little garden snake." (The literal meaning of *innocuous* is "not harmful.")

Now you've got some new words. What are you going to do with them?

5. Put Your New Words to Work at Once

Use them several times the first day you learn them. Say them out loud. Write them in sentences.

Should you "use" them on *friends?* Careful. You don't want them to think you're a stuffed shirt. (It depends on the situation. You *know* when a word sounds natural and when it sounds stuffy.)

How about your *enemies?* You have my blessing. Ask one of them if he's read that article on pneumonoultramicroscopic-silicovolcanoconiosis. (You really can find it in the dictionary.) Now you're one up on him.

So what do you do to improve your vocabulary?

Remember: (1) Try to guess the meaning of the word from the way it's used; (2) look it up; (3) dig the meaning out by the roots; (4) get the powerful prefixes under your belt; (5) put your new words to work at once.

That's all there is to it. You're off on your treasure hunt.

Now do you see why I love words so much?

Aristophanes said, "By words, the mind is excited and the spirit elated." It's as true today as it was when he said it in Athens—*twenty-four hundred years ago.*

I hope you're now like me—hooked on words forever.

Tony Randall

We asked Bill Cosby, who earned his doctorate in education and has been involved in projects which help people learn to read faster, to share what he's learned about reading more in less time.

3

How to Read Faster

by Bill Cosby

When I was a kid in Philadelphia, I must have read every comic book ever published. (There were fewer of them then than there are now.)

I zipped through all of them in a couple of days, then reread the good ones until the next issues arrived.

Yes indeed, when I was a kid, the reading game was a snap.

But as I got older, my eyeballs must have slowed down or something. I mean, comic books started to pile up faster than my brother Russell and I could read them.

It wasn't until much later, when I was getting my doctorate, that I realized it wasn't my eyeballs that were to blame. Thank goodness. They're still moving as well as ever.

The problem is, there's too much to read these days, and too little time to read every word of it.

Now mind you, I still read comic books. In addition to contracts, novels and newspapers. Screenplays, tax returns and correspondence. Even textbooks about how people read, and which techniques help people read more in less time.

I'll let you in on a little secret. There are hundreds of techniques you could learn to help you read faster. But I know of three that are especially good.

And if I can learn them, so can you—and you can put them to use *immediately*.

They are commonsense, practical ways to get the meaning from printed words quickly and efficiently. So you'll have time to enjoy your comic books, have a good laugh with Mark Twain or a good cry with *War and Peace.* Ready?

Okay. The first two ways can help you get through tons of reading material—fast—*without reading every word.*

They'll give you the *overall meaning* of what you're reading and let you cut out an awful lot of *unnecessary* reading.

1. Preview—If It's Long and Hard

Previewing is especially useful for getting a general idea of heavy reading like long magazine or newspaper articles, business reports, and nonfiction books.

It can give you as much as half the comprehension in as little as one tenth the time. For example, you should be able to preview eight or ten 100-page reports in an hour. After previewing, you'll be able to decide which reports (or which *parts* of which reports) are worth a closer look.

Here's how to preview: Read the entire first two paragraphs of whatever you've chosen. Next read only the *first sentence* of each successive paragraph. Then read the entire last two paragraphs.

Previewing doesn't give you all the details. But it does keep you from spending time on things you don't really want—or need—to read.

Notice that previewing gives you a quick, overall view of *long, unfamiliar* material. For short, light reading, there's a better technique.

2. Skim—If It's Short and Simple

Skimming is a good way to get a general idea of light reading, such as popular magazines or the sports and entertainment sections of the paper.

You should be able to skim a weekly popular magazine or

"Learn to read faster and you'll have time for a good laugh with Mark Twain—*and* a good cry with *War and Peace.*"

the second section of your daily paper in less than *half* the time it takes you to read it now.

Skimming is also a great way to review material you've read before.

Here's how to skim: Think of your eyes as magnets. Force them to move fast. Sweep them across each and every line of type. Pick up *only a few key words in each line.*

Everybody skims differently.

You and I may not pick up exactly the same words when we skim the same piece, but we'll both get a pretty similar idea of what it's all about.

To show you how it works, I circled the words I picked out when I skimmed the following story. Try it. It shouldn't take you more than ten seconds.

"Read with a good light—and with as few friends as possible to help you out. No TV, no music. It'll help you concentrate better—*and* read faster."

My brother Russell thinks monsters live in our bedroom closet at night. But I told him he is crazy.

"Go and check then," he said.

I didn't want to. Russell said I was chicken.

"Am not," I said.

"Are so," he said.

So I told him the monsters were going to eat him at midnight. He started to cry. My dad came in and told the monsters to beat it. Then he told us to go to sleep.

"If I hear any more about monsters," he said, "I'll spank you."

We went to (sleep fast.) And you (know something?) They (never did come back.)

Skimming can give you a very good *idea* of this story in about half the words, and in less than half the time it'd take to read every word.

So far, you've seen that previewing and skimming can give you a *general idea* about content—fast. But neither technique can promise more than 50 percent comprehension, because you aren't reading all the words. (Nobody gets something for nothing in the reading game.)

To *read faster and understand most,* if not all, of what you read, you need to know a third technique.

3. *Cluster—to Increase Speed* **and** *Comprehension*

Most of us learned to read by looking at each word in a sentence —*one at a time.*

Like this:

My—brother—Russell—thinks—monsters . . .

You probably still read this way sometimes, especially when the words are difficult. Or when the words have an extraspecial meaning, as in a poem, a Shakespeare play or a contract. And that's okay.

But word-by-word reading is a rotten way to read faster. It actually *cuts down* on your speed.

Clustering trains you to look at *groups* of words instead of one at a time, and it increases your speed enormously. For most of us, clustering is a *totally different way of seeing what we read.*

Here's how to cluster: Train your eyes to see *all* the words in clusters of up to three or four words at a glance.

Here's how I'd cluster the story we just skimmed:

(My brother Russell) (thinks monsters) (live in our bedroom) (closet at night.) (But I told him) (he is crazy.)
("Go and) (check then,") (he said.)
(I didn't want to.) (Russell said) (I was chicken.)
("Am not,") (I said.)

21

"Preview, skim and cluster to read faster—except the things you *want* to read word for word."

"Are so," he said.
So I told him the monsters were going to eat him at midnight. He started to cry. My dad came in and told the monsters to beat it. Then he told us to go to sleep.
"If I hear any more about monsters," he said, "I'll spank you."
We went to sleep fast. And you know something? They never did come back.

Learning to read clusters is not something your eyes do naturally. It takes constant practice.

Here's how to go about it: Pick something light to read. Read it as fast as you can. Concentrate on seeing three to four words at once rather than one word at a time. Then reread the piece at your normal speed to see what you missed the first time.

Try a second piece. First cluster, then reread to see what you missed in this one.

When you can read in clusters without missing much the first time, your speed has increased. Practice fifteen minutes every day and you might pick up the technique in a week or so. (But don't be disappointed if it takes longer. Clustering *every-thing* takes time and practice.)

So now you have three ways to help you read faster. *Preview* to cut down on unnecessary heavy reading. *Skim* to get a quick, general idea of light reading. And *cluster* to increase your speed *and* comprehension.

With enough practice, you'll be able to handle *more* reading at school or work—and at home—*in less time.* You should even have enough time to read your favorite comic books—<u>and</u> *War and Peace!*

We asked Edward T. Thompson to share some of what he has learned about concise writing during his long career—nineteen years of it spent with *Reader's Digest*.

4

How to Write Clearly

by *Edward T. Thompson*

If you are afraid to write, don't be.

If you think you've got to string together big fancy words and high-flying phrases, forget it.

To write well, unless you aspire to be a professional poet or novelist, you only need to get your ideas across simply and clearly.

It's not easy. But it is easier than you might imagine.

There are only three basic requirements:

First, you must *want* to write clearly. And I believe you really do if you've stayed with me this far.

Second, you must be willing to *work hard*. Thinking means work—and that's what it takes to do anything well.

Third, you must know and follow some *basic guidelines*.

If, while you're writing for clarity, some lovely, dramatic or inspired phrases or sentences come to you, fine. Put them in.

But then with cold, objective eyes and mind, ask yourself, "Do they detract from clarity?" If they do, grit your teeth and cut the frills.

'Outline for clarity. Write your points on $3'' \times 5''$ cards—one point to a card. Then you can easily add to, or change the order of points—even delete some."

FOLLOW SOME BASIC GUIDELINES

I can't give you a complete list of do's and don'ts for every writing problem you'll ever face.

But I can give you some fundamental guidelines that cover the most common problems.

1. Outline What You Want to Say

I know that sounds grade-schoolish. But you can't write clearly until, *before you start,* you know where you will stop.

26

Ironically, that's even a problem in writing an outline (i.e., knowing the ending before you begin).

So try this method:

On 3" × 5" cards, write—one point to a card—all the points you need to make.

Divide the cards into piles—one pile for each group of points *closely related* to each other. (If you were describing an automobile, you'd put all the points about mileage in one pile, all the points about safety in another, and so on.)

Arrange your piles of points in a sequence. Which are most important and should be given first or saved for last? Which must you present before others in order to make the others understandable?

Now, *within* each pile, do the same thing: Arrange the *points* in logical, understandable order.

There you have your outline, needing only an introduction and a conclusion.

This is a practical way to outline. It's also flexible. You can add, delete or change the location of points easily.

2. Start Where Your Readers Are

How much do they know about the subject? Don't write to a level higher than your readers' knowledge of it.

CAUTION: Forget that old—and wrong—advice about writing to a twelve-year-old mentality. That's insulting. But do remember that your prime purpose is to *explain* something, not prove that you're smarter than your readers.

3. Avoid Jargon

Don't use words, expressions, phrases known only to people with specific knowledge or interests.

Example: A scientist, using scientific jargon, wrote, "The

"Writing clearly means avoiding jargon. He
could have said, 'All the fish died.' "

biota exhibited a one hundred percent mortality response." He
could have written, "All the fish died."

4. Use Familiar Combinations of Words

A speech writer for President Franklin D. Roosevelt wrote, "We
are endeavoring to construct a more inclusive society." FDR
changed it to, "We're going to make a country in which no one is
left out."

CAUTION: By familiar combinations of words, I do *not* mean
incorrect grammar. *That* can be *un*clear. Example: John's father
says he can't go out Friday. (Who can't go out? John or his
father?)

5. Use "First-degree" Words

These words immediately bring an image to your mind. Other
words must be "translated" through the first-degree word before you see the image. Those are second/third-degree words.

First-degree words	Second/third-degree words
face	visage, countenance
stay	abide, remain, reside
book	volume, tome, publication

First-degree words are usually the most precise words, too.

6. Stick to the Point

Your outline, which was more work in the beginning, now saves you work. Because now you can ask about any sentence you write: "Does it relate to a point in the outline? If it doesn't, should I add it to the outline? If not, I'm getting off the track." Then, full steam ahead—on the main line.

7. Be as Brief as Possible

Whatever you write, shortening—*condensing*—almost always makes it tighter, straighter, easier to read and understand.

Condensing, as *Reader's Digest* does it, is in large part artistry. But it involves techniques that anyone can learn and use.

Present your points in logical ABC order. Here again, your outline should save you work because, if you did it right, your points already stand in logical ABC order: A makes B understandable, B makes C understandable and so on. To write in a straight line is to say something clearly in the fewest possible words.

Don't waste words telling people what they already know. Notice how we edited this:

"Have you ever wondered how banks rate you as a credit risk? ~~You know, of course, that it's some combination of facts about your income, your job and so on. But actually,~~ many banks have a scoring system. . . ."

Cut out excess evidence and unnecessary anecdotes. Usually, one fact or example (at most, two) will support a point. More just

"Grit your teeth and cut the frills. That's one of the suggestions I offer here to help you write clearly. They cover the most common problems. And they're all easy to follow."

belabor it. And while writing about something may remind you of a good story, ask yourself, "Does it *really help* to tell the story, or does it slow me down?"

(Many people think *Reader's Digest* articles are filled with anecdotes. Actually, we always used them sparingly and usually for one of two reasons: Either the subject is so dry it needs some "humanity" to give it life; or the subject is so hard to grasp, it needs anecdotes to help readers understand. If the subject is both lively and easy to grasp, you should move right along.)

Look for the most common word wasters: windy phrases.

30

Windy phrases ————————	Cut to . . .
at the present time ———————	now
in the event of —————————	if
in the majority of instances ———	usually

Look for passive verbs you can make active. Invariably, this produces a shorter sentence. "The cherry tree *was* chopped down by George Washington." (Passive verb and nine words.) "George Washington *chopped* down the cherry tree." (Active verb and seven words.)

Look for positive/negative sections from which you can cut the negative. See how we did it here:

"The answer ~~does not rest with carelessness or incompetence. It lies largely in~~ having enough people to do the job."

Finally, to write more clearly by saying it in fewer words: When you've finished, stop.

Edward T. Thompson

We asked Kurt Vonnegut, author of such novels as *Slaughterhouse-Five, Deadeye Dick* and *Cat's Cradle,* to tell you how to put your style and personality into everything you write.

5

How to Write with Style

by Kurt Vonnegut

Newspaper reporters and technical writers are trained to reveal almost nothing about themselves in their writings. This makes them freaks in the world of writers, since almost all of the other ink-stained wretches in that world reveal a lot about themselves to readers. We call these revelations, accidental and intentional, elements of style.

These revelations tell us as readers what sort of person it is with whom we are spending time. Does the writer sound ignorant or informed, stupid or bright, crooked or honest, humorless or playful—? And on and on.

Why should you examine your writing style with the idea of improving it? Do so as a mark of respect for your readers, whatever you're writing. If you scribble your thoughts any which way, your readers will surely feel that you care nothing about them. They will mark you down as an egomaniac or a chowderhead— or, worse, they will stop reading you.

The most damning revelation you can make about yourself is that you do not know what is interesting and what is not. Don't you yourself like or dislike writers mainly for what they choose to show you or make you think about? Did you ever admire an empty-headed writer for his or her mastery of the language? No.

So your own winning style must begin with ideas in your head.

"Pick a subject you care so deeply about that you'd speak on a soapbox about it."

I. Find a Subject You Care About

Find a subject you care about and which you in your heart feel others should care about. It is this genuine caring, and not your games with language, which will be the most compelling and seductive element in your style.

I am not urging you to write a novel, by the way—although I would not be sorry if you wrote one, provided you genuinely cared about something. A petition to the mayor about a pothole in front of your house or a love letter to the girl next door will do.

2. *Do Not Ramble, Though*

I won't ramble on about that.

3. *Keep It Simple*

As for your use of language: Remember that two great masters of language, William Shakespeare and James Joyce, wrote sentences which were almost childlike when their subjects were most profound. "To be or not to be?" asks Shakespeare's Hamlet. The longest word is three letters long. Joyce, when he was frisky, could put together a sentence as intricate and as glittering as a necklace for Cleopatra, but my favorite sentence in his short story "Eveline" is this one: "She was tired." At that point in the story, no other words could break the heart of a reader as those three words do.

Simplicity of language is not only reputable, but perhaps even sacred. The Bible opens with a sentence well within the writing skills of a lively fourteen-year-old: "In the beginning God created the heaven and the earth."

4. *Have the Guts to Cut*

It may be that you, too, are capable of making necklaces for Cleopatra, so to speak. But your eloquence should be the servant of the ideas in your head. Your rule might be this: If a sentence, no matter how excellent, does not illuminate your subject in some new and useful way, scratch it out.

5. *Sound like Yourself*

The writing style which is most natural for you is bound to echo the speech you heard when a child. English was the novelist Joseph Conrad's third language, and much that seems piquant in his use of English was no doubt colored by his first language,

"Be merciless on yourself. If a sentence does not illuminate your subject in some new and useful way, scratch it out."

which was Polish. And lucky indeed is the writer who has grown up in Ireland, for the English spoken there is so amusing and musical. I myself grew up in Indianapolis, where common speech sounds like a band saw cutting galvanized tin, and employs a vocabulary as unornamental as a monkey wrench.

In some of the more remote hollows of Appalachia, children still grow up hearing songs and locutions of Elizabethan times. Yes, and many Americans grow up hearing a language other than English, or an English dialect a majority of Americans cannot understand.

All these varieties of speech are beautiful, just as the varieties of butterflies are beautiful. No matter what your first language, you should treasure it all your life. If it happens not to be standard English, and if it shows itself when you write standard English, the result is usually delightful, like a very pretty girl with one eye that is green and one that is blue.

I myself find that I trust my own writing most, and others seem to trust it most, too, when I sound most like a person from Indianapolis, which is what I am. What alternatives do I have? The one most vehemently recommended by teachers has no doubt been pressed on you, as well: to write like cultivated Englishmen of a century or more ago.

6. Say What You Mean to Say

I used to be exasperated by such teachers, but am no more. I understand now that all those antique essays and stories with which I was to compare my own work were not magnificent for their datedness or foreignness, but for saying precisely what their authors meant them to say. My teachers wished me to write accurately, always selecting the most effective words, and relating the words to one another unambiguously, rigidly, like parts of a machine. The teachers did not want to turn me into an Englishman after all. They hoped that I would become understandable—and therefore understood. And there went my dream of doing with words what Pablo Picasso did with paint or what any number of jazz idols did with music. If I broke all the rules of punctuation, had words mean whatever I wanted them to mean, and strung them together higgledy-piggledy, I would simply not be understood. So you, too, had better avoid Picasso-style or jazz-style writing if you have something worth saying and wish to be understood.

Readers want our pages to look very much like pages they have seen before. Why? This is because they themselves have a tough job to do, and they need all the help they can get from us.

7. *Pity the Readers*

Readers have to identify thousands of little marks on paper, and make sense of them immediately. They have to read, an art so difficult that most people don't really master it even after having studied it all through grade school and high school—twelve long years.

So this discussion must finally acknowledge that our stylistic options as writers are neither numerous nor glamorous, since our readers are bound to be such imperfect artists. Our audience requires us to be sympathetic and patient teachers, ever willing to simplify and clarify, whereas we would rather soar high above the crowd, singing like nightingales.

That is the bad news. The good news is that we Americans are governed under a unique constitution, which allows us to write whatever we please without fear of punishment. So the most meaningful aspect of our styles, which is what we choose to write about, is utterly unlimited.

8. *For Really Detailed Advice*

For a discussion of literary style in a narrower sense, a more technical sense, I commend to your attention *The Elements of Style,* by William Strunk, Jr., and E. B. White. E. B. White is, of course, one of the most admirable literary stylists this country has so far produced.

You should realize, too, that no one would care how well or badly Mr. White expressed himself if he did not have perfectly enchanting things to say.

We asked Pulitzer Prize-winning novelist James A. Michener, author of *Tales of the South Pacific, Centennial, The Covenant* and *Space,* to tell how you can benefit from the most helpful service in your community.

6

How to Use a Library

by James A. Michener

You're driving your car home from work or school. And something goes wrong. The engine stalls out at lights, or holds back as you go to pass another car.

It needs a tune-up—and soon. Where do you go? The library.

You can take out an auto repair manual that tells step-by-step how to tune up your make and model.

Or your tennis game has fallen off. You've lost your touch at the net. Where do you go?

The library—for a few books on improving your tennis form.

"The library!" you say. "That's where my teacher sends me to do—ugh—homework."

Unfortunately, I've found that's exactly the way many people feel. If you're among them, you're denying yourself the easiest way to improve yourself, enjoy yourself and even cope with life.

It's hard for me to imagine what I would be doing today if I had not fallen in love, at the ripe old age of seven, with the Melinda Cox Library in my hometown of Doylestown, Pennsylvania. At our house we just could not afford books. The books in that free library would change my life dramatically.

Who knows what your library can open up for you?

My first suggestion for making the most of your library is to do what I did: Read and read and read. For pleasure—and for understanding.

How to Kick the TV Habit

If it's TV that keeps you from cultivating this delicious habit, I can offer a sure remedy. Take home from the library a stack of books that might look interesting.

Pile them on the TV set. Next time you are tempted to turn on a program you really don't want to see, reach for a book instead.

Over the years, some people collect a mental list of books they mean to read. If you don't have such a list, here is a suggestion. Take from the library some of the books you might have enjoyed dramatized on TV, like Erich Maria Remarque's *All Quiet on the Western Front,* James Clavell's *Shōgun,* J. R. R. Tolkien's *The Hobbit* or Victor Hugo's *"Les Misérables."*

"You don't have to go this far to cut back on the TV habit and enjoy reading more. See my suggestions here."

"Every time I go to the library, I make a beeline to the card catalog. Learn to use it. It's easy."

If you like what you read, you can follow up with other satisfying books by the same authors.

Some people in their reading limit themselves to current talked-about bestsellers. Oh, what they miss! The library is full of yesterday's bestsellers; and they still make compelling reading today. Some that I've enjoyed: A. B. Guthrie's *The Big Sky,* Carl Van Doren's *Benjamin Franklin,* Mari Sandoz's *Old Jules* and Norman Mailer's *The Naked and the Dead.*

How do you find these or any other books you're looking for? It's easy—with the card catalog.

Learn to Use the Card Catalog

Every time I go to the library—and I go more than once a week —I invariably make a beeline to the card catalog before anything else. It's the nucleus of any public library.

43

"I discover all kinds of interesting books just by browsing in the stacks. I encourage you to browse."

The card catalog lists every book in the library by:
1. author; 2. title; 3. subject.

Let's pick an interesting subject to look up. I have always been fascinated by astronomy.

You'll be surprised at the wealth of material you will find under "Astronomy" to draw upon. And the absorbing books you didn't know existed on it.

CAUTION: Always have a pencil and paper when you use the card catalog. Once you jot down the numbers of the books you are interested in, you are ready to find them on the shelves.

Learn to Use the Stacks

Libraries call the shelves "the stacks." In many smaller libraries which you'll be using, the stacks will be open for you to browse.

To me there is a special thrill in tracking down the books I want in the stacks. For invariably, I find books about which I knew nothing, and these often turn out to be the very ones I need. You will find the same thing happening to you when you start to browse in the stacks. "A learned mind is the end product of browsing."

CAUTION: If you take a book from the stacks to your work desk, do not try to return it to its proper place. That's work for the experts. If you replace it incorrectly, the next seeker won't be able to find it.

Learn to Know the Reference Librarian

Some of the brightest and best-informed men and women in America are the librarians who specialize in providing reference help.

Introduce yourself. State your problem. And be amazed at how much help you will receive.

CAUTION: Don't waste the time of this expert by asking silly questions you ought to answer yourself. Save the reference librarian for the really big ones.

Learn to Use the Reader's Guide to Periodical Literature

This green-bound index is one of the most useful items in any library. It indexes all the articles in the major magazines, including newspaper magazine supplements.

Thus it provides a guide to the very latest expert information on any subject that interests you.

So if you want to do a really first-class job, find out which magazines your library subscribes to, then consult the *Reader's Guide* and track down recent articles on your subject. When you use this wonderful tool effectively, you show the mark of a real scholar.

Four Personal Hints

Since you can take most books home, but not magazines, take full notes when using the latter.

Many libraries today provide a reprographic machine that can quickly copy pages you need from magazines and books. Ask about it.

If you are working on a project of some size which will require repeated library visits, keep a small notebook in which you record the identification numbers of the books you will be using frequently. This will save you valuable time, because you won't have to consult the card catalog or search aimlessly through the stacks each time you visit for material you seek.

Some of the very best books in any library are the reference books, which may not be taken home. Learn what topics they cover and how best to use them, for these books are wonderful repositories of human knowledge.

In today's TV world, many people never get a chance to be bitten by the reading bug. To me that's a shame. But even if you don't read for pleasure, it's an even bigger shame if you don't take advantage of the other things a library can offer to help you in your busy life.

Unexpected Help

Do you know some of the unexpected things your library can help you do? Here's a sample:

Learn welding. Or almost any trade or skill with the how-to books from your library.

Get tips on local jobs. Check weekly postings in your library.

Borrow the latest dress patterns. Many libraries lend them out.

Type up a résumé. Or a letter to a prospective employer. Most libraries will let you use a typewriter for any worthwhile purpose.

Look up the address of a friend across the country. Telephone operators won't give you addresses. So most libraries collect phone books for major American cities.

Pull a rabbit out of a hat. Read how in Walter Gibson's *Encyclopedia of Magic and Conjuring.*

Listen to a book. Borrow *Moby Dick*—or even a current bestseller—on audiocassette. Hear a book while you're driving, or painting the living room.

Your library can give you basic help on *any* subject.

Your Business and Legal Adviser

Your library can give you help on any subject. It can even be your business and legal adviser.

How many times have you scratched your head over how to get a tax rebate on your summer job? You'll find answers in tax guides at the library. Thinking of buying or renting a house? You'll find guides to that. Want to defend yourself in traffic court? Find out how in legal books at the library.

Your Entertainment and Arts Center

Live concerts: If you drop in at the library on certain evenings and hear the strains of a Beethoven string quartet or "Paperback Writer," don't be surprised. More and more libraries are becoming halls for free concerts and lectures.

Free movies: Your library shows recent and classic films regularly. You can see them there or take them home to show your family.

Free prints: Would you like to hang great paintings on your walls at home? Borrow framed prints from the library. Replace them in a few weeks with others. I have a friend who has a favorite he goes back for every six months.

Library Projects Can Be Fun—and Rewarding

Here are a few ideas:

1. *What are your roots?* Trace your ancestors. Many libraries specialize in genealogy.

2. *Did George Washington sleep nearby?* Or Billy the Kid? Your library's collection of local history books can put you on the trail.

3. *Cook a Polynesian feast.* Or an ancient Roman banquet. Read how in the library's cookbooks.

4. *Take up photography.* Check the library for consumer reviews of cameras before you buy. Take out books on lighting, composition, or darkroom techniques.

Or—you name it!

If you haven't detected by now my enthusiasm for libraries, let me offer two personal notes.

I'm particularly pleased that in recent years two beautiful libraries have been named after me: a small community library in Quakertown, Pennsylvania, and the huge research library at the University of Northern Colorado in Greeley.

And I like libraries so much that I married a librarian.

James A. Michener

We asked Steve Allen, television comedian, composer, writer of the television series "Meeting of Minds," author of numerous books and lover of the classics, to tell how you can appreciate Western man's greatest written works.

7

How to Enjoy the Classics

by Steve Allen

Why is it? In school we learn one of the most amazing and difficult feats man has ever accomplished—*how to read*—and at the same time we learn to hate to read the things worth reading most.

It's happened to us all—with assignment reading. It happened to me. The teacher assigned *Moby Dick*. I didn't want to read it. So I fought it. I disliked it. I thought I won.

But I lost. My struggle to keep at arm's length from *Moby Dick* cost me all the good things that can come from learning to come to terms with those special few books we call the "classics."

I've come back to *Moby Dick* on my own since. I *like* it. And I've discovered a new level of pleasure from it with each reading.

What *is* a classic? A classic is a book that gives you that exhilarating feeling, if only for a moment, that you've finally uncovered part of the meaning of life.

A classic is a book that's stood the test of time, that men and women all over the world keep reaching for throughout the ages for its special enlightenment.

Not many books can survive such a test. Considering all

the volumes that have been produced since man first put chisel to stone, classics account for an infinitesimal share of the total— less than .001 percent. That's just a few thousand books. Of those, under a hundred make up the solid core.

Why should you tackle the classics? Why try to enjoy them? I've got three good reasons:

1. Classics open up your mind.
2. Classics help you grow.
3. Classics help you understand life, your world, yourself.

That last one is the big one. A classic can give you insights into yourself that you will get nowhere else. Sure, you can get pleasure out of almost any book. But a classic, once you penetrate it, lifts you up *high*. Aeschylus's *Oresteia* was written nearly twenty-five hundred years ago—and it still knocks me out.

Chaucer, who wrote *The Canterbury Tales,* claimed he learned about love by reading the classics of his day rather than under the moonlight. (Having read *The Canterbury Tales,* I don't know if I believe him.)

But I can hear you saying, "I've *tried* reading the classics. They're hard to understand. I can't get into them."

Let me offer some suggestions that will help you open up this wondrous world.

Before I do, here's a warning. Don't read the classics just to show off. You'll turn others off if you go around trying to impress people with, "As Emerson so aptly put it . . ."

With that off my chest, let's go. Pick up a classic you've always promised to try. Then take Dr. Allen's advice.

1. Know the Kind of Book You're Getting Into

Is it a novel, drama, biography, epic poem, philosophy, history? It helps to know. To find out, check the table of contents, read the book cover or the preface, or look up the title or author in *The Reader's Encyclopedia.*

2. Don't Read in Bed

Classics can be tough going. I'll admit it. You need to be alert, with all your senses sharp. When you read in bed, you're courting sleep—and you'll blame it on the book when you start nodding off.

3. Read the Author's Preface First
—but Not Somebody Else's

The author wrote it to help you get into his book. Someone else's preface will bore you, because he's read the book and you haven't. And he'll be trying to discuss characters, plots and ideas you don't know anything about. Save this for afterward when *you'll* be anxious to share what you've just read.

4. Don't Let a Lot of Characters Throw You

Dostoevsky tosses fifty major characters at you in *The Brothers Karamazov*. In the very first chapter of *War and Peace* Tolstoy bombards you with twenty-two names—long, complicated ones like Anna Pavlovna Scherer and Prince Andrey Bolkonski. Don't scurry for cover. The characters will gradually sort themselves out and you'll feel as comfortable with them as you do with your own dear friends who were strangers too when you met them.

5. Give the Author a Chance

Don't say "I don't get it!" too soon. Keep reading right to the end. To understand some classics, you might have to read them a second and a third time.

Sometimes, though, you may not be ready for the book you're trying to get into. I tackled Plato's *Republic* three times before it finally opened up to me. And, man, was it worth it! So if

"Some of my best friends come out of the pages of the classics I suggest to you here. They'll be your best friends, too, for they'll help you better understand your life, your world and yourself."

you really can't make a go of the book in your lap, put it aside for another day, or year, and take on another one. There are plenty.

6. Read at Different Speeds

Set your pace depending on what you read. During dialogue, read it as you'd hear it. During narrative and some description, you can charge ahead more quickly. *Re*read the parts that wrinkle your brow—*and* the ones that especially delight you.

7. Read in Big Bites

Don't read in short nibbles. How can you expect to get your head into anything that way? Take big bites. The longer you stay with it, the more you get into the rhythm and mood, and the more pleasure you get from it.

When you're reading *Zorba the Greek,* you might try putting bouzouki music on the record player; Proust, a little Debussy; Shakespeare, Elizabethan theater music.

8. Read What the Author Read

To better understand where the author is coming from, as we say, read the books he once read and that impressed him. Shakespeare, for example, dipped into Thomas North's translation of *Plutarch's Lives* for *Julius Caesar, Antony and Cleopatra* and *A Midsummer Night's Dream.* It's fun to know you're reading what *he* read.

9. Read About the Author's Time

You are the product of your time. Any author is the product of *his* time. Knowing at least something of the history of that time, the problems that he and others faced, their attitudes, will help you understand the author's point of view. *Important point:* You may not agree with the author. No problem. At least he's made you think.

10. Read About the Author's Life

The more you know about an author's own experiences, the more you'll understand why he wrote what he wrote. You'll begin to see the autobiographical odds and ends hidden in his work. A writer can't help but reveal himself. In *Leaves of Grass,* Walt Whitman said, "This is no book. Who touches this touches a man."

Most of our surmises about Shakespeare's life come from clues found in his plays.

11. Read the Book Again

All classics bear rereading. If after you finish the book you're intrigued but still confused, reread it then and there. It'll open up some more to you.

If you did read a classic a few years back and loved it, read it again. The book will have so many new things to say to you, you'll hardly believe it's the same one.

A Few Classics to Enjoy

You can find an excellent list of the basic classics compiled by Clifton Fadiman in his *Lifetime Reading Plan;* and you can find fine collections of the classics themselves, like *The Harvard Classics* and Mortimer J. Adler's *Great Books* program. Look into them.

Before you do, I'd like to suggest a few classics that can light up your life. Even though some might have been spoiled for you by the required-reading stigma, try them. Try them. And *try* them.

1. Homer: *Iliad* and *Odyssey.* The Adam and Eve of Western literature. People have been thrilling to them for nearly three thousand years. One an exciting epic of war, complete with Achilles' heel and Helen of Troy; the other the greatest travel adventure story of all time, complete with Circe and Cyclops.

Read a good recent translation. My favorite is by Robert Fitzgerald.

2. François Rabelais: *Gargantua and Pantagruel.* Stupendous stuff by a man bursting with the force of the Renaissance. A passionate love of life comes through this sidesplitting story of two giants, first Gargantua, then his son Pantagruel, as they make love and war in sixteenth-century France. My description of the book comes ultimately from Rabelais: *gargantuan!* I recommend the robust Samuel Putnam translation.

3. Geoffrey Chaucer: *The Canterbury Tales.* Chaucer was the first great writer to write in English. Others of his time still wrote

in Latin. He wrote for the ordinary person with simplicity, delight and delicious humor. The stories revolve around thirty people swapping whoppers on the sixty-mile, four-day pilgrimage from Southwark to the Shrine of Thomas à Becket in Canterbury six centuries ago. The best tales: "The Miller's Tale," "The Reeve's Tale," "The Wife of Bath's Tale." Don't be surprised if the people you meet here are like people you know in *your* life.

4. Miguel de Cervantes: *Don Quixote.* The heroically foolish old Don with his "impossible dream" takes on a rough-and-tumble world.

This book is a protest against affectation. It pits the old against the new, reality against fantasy. It's the first modern novel and still by far the best. How could you go through life without reading it once?

5. William Shakespeare: Plays. Am I lucky. So are you. We can enjoy Shakespeare in the original language—ours, English. So we can get all the pleasure of his use of words—just as those who read Dante's *The Divine Comedy* can, reading it in Italian.

Shakespeare turned out thirty-seven plays. Some are failures, some are great. All offer gold. His best: *Hamlet, Macbeth* and *Romeo and Juliet.*

TIP 1. Find an edition of his plays that spells out the names of characters speaking. Not HAM., GUIL., ROS. or POL., but HAMLET, GUILDENSTERN, ROSENCRANTZ and POLONIUS. This way you can concentrate your brainpower on what they're saying rather than on who's saying it.

TIP 2. When you read Shakespeare, don't do it the way you had to in school, pausing every three seconds to look up strange words and arcane phrases. Don't stop. Keep on reading to the end. Once you get the rhythm, you'll suddenly begin to understand Shakespeare's language.

TIP 3. Act out the plays in your mind. *Hear* the characters talk. See them move on the stage. Shakespeare left no stage directions to speak of, so it's all up to you. Be a producer! Put on your own show in your head.

6. Jonathan Swift: *Travels into Several Remote Nations of the*

World . . . by Lemuel Gulliver. Better known as *Gulliver's Travels.* Maybe you read a children's version once. This is nothing like that. Swift wrote it to "vex the world rather than divert it." Despite himself, he diverted it. Lilliput is astonishingly like England in Swift's day. A ruthless book that shows how foolish we all can be. Even you and I.

7. Daniel Defoe: *Robinson Crusoe.* This is not a children's book either. It's a fake memoir palmed off as true. Defoe, who never visited the West Indies or the Pacific, achieved what seems complete realism by spinning out fascinating details of how Crusoe ate, hunted, survived and created his private castaway world.

8. Charles Dickens: *The Pickwick Papers.* No one can breathe life into characters the way Dickens can. Especially the inimitable Samuel Pickwick, Esq. Edmund Wilson called Dickens "the greatest dramatic writer the English had had since Shakespeare." And said "he created the largest and most varied world."

9. Herman Melville: *Moby Dick.* Like *Don Quixote, Gulliver's Travels* and *Huckleberry Finn,* this work can be interpreted on two or more levels. It's about whaling. It's about evil. It's about mankind's fiercest fears and desires. D. H. Lawrence said, "It moves awe in the soul." Moby Dick could have been written only by an American.

10. Mark Twain: *The Adventures of Huckleberry Finn.* Maybe you had to read this one in school. Well, climb back on that raft with Huck and Jim. You'll find new meaning this time. Mark Twain (really Samuel Clemens) grew up in the frontier town of Hannibal, Missouri (pop. 500). He hated injustice and oppression. He was the first to use American lingo at the level of high art. Hemingway said, "All modern American literature comes from *Huckleberry Finn.*"

11. Fyodor Dostoevsky: *The Brothers Karamazov.* Sigmund Freud called this book "the most magnificent novel ever written." It's a detective story, a romance, a melodrama, a mystery

"*Moby Dick* escaped me when it was assigned reading. I've landed it since and loved it. Don't let assigned reading spoil the classics for you."

play—with some pyrotechnic philosophizing that will separate the men from the boys. It was meant to have a sequel. (Brothers II?) He never lived to write it. I wish he had.

12. James Joyce: *Portrait of the Artist as a Young Man*. This is the story of the gestation of a human soul, that of Stephen Dedalus, who pops up later in Joyce's blockbuster, *Ulysses*. Some writers write visually. Joyce, an Irishman in love with his lilting language, wrote for the ear. It'll open your eyes.

These few suggestions, of course, hardly scratch the surface.

Now I'm going to stick my neck out and suggest a few more-recent books that I think might become classics someday: Ernest Hemingway, *For Whom the Bell Tolls;* Nikos Kazantzakis, *Zorba the Greek;* Alan Paton, *Cry, the Beloved Country;* Joseph Heller,

Catch-22; Alexandr Solzhenitsyn, *The Gulag Archipelago.* Give them a try.

Because of considerations of space, I've had to limit myself to the works of Western man. According to some, the greatest novel in the world is from Japan: *The Tale of Genji* by Lady Murasaki. The greatest love story is from China: *The Dream of the Red Chamber* by Hsueh-Chin Tsao. Both are available here in good English translations. *Plunge right in.*

Don't just dip your toe into the deep waters of the classics. Plunge in! Like generations upon generations of bright human beings before you, you'll find yourself invigorated to the marrow by the thoughts and observations of the most gifted writers in history.

You still enjoy looking at classic paintings. You enjoy hearing classical music. Good books will hold you, too.

Someone has said that the classics are the diary of man. Open up the diary. Read about yourself—and *understand* yourself.

Steve Allen

We asked Jane Bryant Quinn, syndicated newspaper columnist, business commentator for the CBS-TV News, columnist for *Newsweek* and authority on getting a grip on personal finance, to tell how anyone can understand and profit from a company's annual report.

8

How to Read an Annual Report

by Jane Bryant Quinn

To some business people I know, curling up with a good annual report is almost more exciting than getting lost in John Le Carré's latest spy thriller.

But to you it might be another story. "Who needs that?" I can hear you ask. *You* do—if you're going to gamble any of your future *working* for a company, *investing* in it, or *selling* to it.

Why Should You Bother?

Say you've got a job interview at Galactic Industries. Well, what does the company do? Does its future look good? Or will the next recession leave your part of the business on the beach?

Or say you're thinking of investing your own hard-earned money in its stock. Sales are up. But are its profits getting better or worse?

Or say you're going to supply it with a lot of parts. Should you extend Galactic plenty of credit or keep it on a short leash?

How to Get One

You'll find answers in its annual report. Where do you find *that?* Your library should have the annual reports of nearby companies plus leading national ones. It also has listings of companies' financial officers and their addresses so you can write for annual reports.

So now Galactic Industries' latest annual report is sitting in front of you ready to be cracked. How do you crack it?

Where do we start? *Not* at the front. At the *back*. We don't want to be surprised at the end of *this* story.

Start at the Back

First, turn back to the report of the *certified public accountant.* This third-party auditor will tell you right off the bat if Galactic's report conforms with "generally accepted accounting principles."

Watch out for the words "subject to." They mean the financial report is clean *only* if you take the company's word about a particular piece of business, and the accountant isn't sure you should. Doubts like this are usually settled behind closed doors.

"Reading an annual report can be (almost) as exciting as a spy thriller—*if* you know how to find the clues. I'll show you how to find the most important ones here."

When a "subject to" makes it into the annual report, it could mean trouble.

What else should you know before you check the numbers?

Stay in the back of the book and go to the *footnotes.* Yep! The whole profits story is sometimes in the footnotes.

Are earnings down? If it's only because of a change in accounting, maybe that's good. The company owes less tax and has more money in its pocket. Are earnings up? Maybe that's bad. They may be up because of a special windfall that won't happen again next year. The footnotes know.

For What Happened and Why

Now turn to the *letter from the chairman.* Usually addressed "To our stockholders," it's up front, and *should* be in more ways than one. The chairman's tone reflects the personality, the well-being of his company.

In his letter he should tell you how his company fared this year. But more important, he should tell you *why.* Keep an eye out for sentences that start with "Except for . . ." and "Despite the . . ." They're clues to problems.

Insights into the Future

On the positive side, a chairman's letter should give you insights into the company's future and its *stance* on economic or political trends that may affect it.

While you're up front, look for what's new in each line of business. Is management getting the company in good shape to weather the tough and competitive years ahead?

Now—and no sooner—should you dig into the numbers.

One source is the *balance sheet.* It is a snapshot of how the company stands at a single point in time. On the left are *assets*— everything the company owns. Things that can quickly be turned into cash are *current assets.* On the right are *liabilities*—everything the company owes. *Current liabilities* are the debts due in one year, which are paid out of current assets.

The difference between current assets and current liabilities is *net working capital,* a key figure to watch from one annual (and quarterly) report to another. If working capital shrinks, it could mean trouble. One possibility: The company may not be able to keep dividends growing rapidly.

Look for Growth Here

Stockholders' equity is the difference between total assets and liabilities. It is the presumed dollar value of what stockholders own. You want it to grow.

Another important number to watch is *long-term debt.* High and rising debt, relative to equity, may be no problem for a growing business. But it shows weakness in a company that's leveling out. (More on that later.)

The second basic source of numbers is the *income statement.* It shows how much money Galactic made or lost over the year.

Most people look at one figure first. It's in the income statement at the bottom: *net earnings per share.* Watch out. It can fool you. Galactic's management could boost earnings by selling off a plant. Or by cutting the budget for research and advertising. (See the footnotes.) So don't be smug about net earnings until you've found out how they happened—and how they might happen next year.

Check Net Sales First

The number you *should* look at first in the income statement is *net sales.* Ask yourself: Are sales going *up at a faster rate* than the last time around? When sales increases start to slow, the company may be in trouble. Also ask: Have sales gone up faster than inflation? If not, the company's *real* sales may be behind. And ask yourself once more: Have sales gone down because the company is selling off a losing business? If so, profits may be soaring.

(I never promised you that figuring out an annual report was going to be *easy.*)

Get Out Your Calculator

Another important thing to study today is the company's debt. Get out your pocket calculator, and turn to the balance sheet. Divide long-term liabilities by stockholders' equity. That's the *debt-to-equity ratio.*

A high ratio means that the company borrows a lot of money to spark its growth. That's okay—*if* sales grow, too, and *if* there's enough cash on hand to meet the payments. A company doing well on borrowed money can earn big profits for its stockholders. But if sales fall, watch out. The whole enterprise may slowly sink. Some companies can handle high ratios, others can't.

You Have to Compare

That brings up the most important thing of all: *One* annual report, *one* chairman's letter, *one* ratio won't tell you much. You have to compare. Is the company's debt-to-equity ratio better or worse than it used to be? Better or worse than the industry norms? Better or worse, after this recession, than it was after the last recession? In company-watching, *comparisons are all.* They tell you if management is staying on top of things.

Financial analysts work out many other ratios to tell them how the company is doing. You can learn more about them from books on the subject. Ask your librarian.

But one thing you will never learn from an annual report is how much to pay for a company's stock. Galactic may be running well. But if investors expected it to run better, the stock might fall. Or, Galactic could be slumping badly. But if investors see a better day tomorrow, the stock could rise.

"For inside information, an annual report is second only to meeting with the brass behind closed doors. Come on in."

Two Important Suggestions

Those are some basics for weighing a company's health from its annual report. But if you want to know all you can about a company, you need to do a little more homework. First, see what the business press has been saying about it over recent years. Again, ask your librarian.

Finally, you should keep up with what's going on in business, economics and politics here and around the world. All can —and will—affect you and the companies you're interested in.

Each year companies give you more and more information

in their annual reports. Profiting from that information is up to you. I hope you profit from mine.

Jane Bryant Quinn

We asked George Plimpton, who writes books about facing the sports pros (such as *Paper Lion* and *Shadow Box),* and who's in demand to speak about it, to tell you how to face the fear of making a speech.

9

How to Make a Speech

by George Plimpton

One of life's terrors for the uninitiated is to be asked to make a speech.

"Why me?" will probably be your first reaction. "I don't have anything to say." It should be reassuring (though it rarely is) that since you were asked, somebody must think you do. The fact is that each one of us has a store of material which should be of interest to others. There is no reason why it should not be adapted to a speech.

Why Know How to Speak?

Scary as it is, it's important for anyone to be able to speak in front of others, whether twenty around a conference table or a hall filled with a thousand faces.

Being able to speak can mean better grades in any class. It can mean talking the town council out of increasing your property taxes. It can mean talking top management into buying your plan.

How to Pick a Topic

You were probably asked to speak in the first place in the hope that you would be able to articulate a topic that you know something about. Still, it helps to find out about your audience first. Who are they? Why are they there? What are they interested in? How much do they already know about your subject? One kind of talk would be appropriate for the Women's Club of Columbus, Ohio, and quite another for the guests at the Vince Lombardi dinner.

How to Plan What to Say

Here is where you must do your homework.

The more you sweat in advance, the less you'll have to sweat once you appear on stage. Research your topic thoroughly. Check the library for facts, quotes, books and timely magazine and newspaper articles on your subject. Get in touch with experts. Write to them, make phone calls, get interviews to help round out your material.

In short, gather—and learn—far more than you'll ever use. You can't imagine how much confidence that knowledge will inspire.

Now start organizing and writing. Most authorities suggest that a good speech breaks down into three basic parts: an introduction, the body of the speech, and the summation.

Introduction: An audience makes up its mind very quickly. Once the mood of an audience is set, it is difficult to change it, which is why introductions are important. If the speech is to be lighthearted in tone, the speaker can start off by telling a good-natured story about the subject or himself.

But be careful of jokes, especially the shaggy-dog variety. For some reason, the joke that convulses guests in a living room tends to suffer as it emerges through the amplifying system into a public gathering place.

Main body: There are four main intents in the body of the well-made speech. These are (1) to entertain, which is probably the hardest; (2) to instruct, which is the easiest if the speaker has done the research and knows the subject; (3) to persuade, which one does at a sales presentation, a political rally, or a town meeting; and finally, (4) to inspire, which is what the speaker emphasizes at a sales meeting, in a sermon, or at a pep rally. ("Hurry Up" Yost, the onetime Michigan football coach, gave such an inspiration-filled halftime talk that he got carried away and at the final exhortation led his team on the run through the wrong locker-room door into the swimming pool.

Summation: This is where you should "ask for the order." An ending should probably incorporate a sentence or two which sounds like an ending—a short summary of the main points of the speech, perhaps, or the repeat of a phrase that most embodies what the speaker has hoped to convey. It is valuable to think of the last sentence or two as something which might produce applause. Phrases which are perfectly appropriate to signal this are: "In closing . . ." or "I have one last thing to say. . . ."

Once done—fully written, or the main points set down on $3'' \times 5''$ index cards—the next problem is the actual presentation of the speech. Ideally, a speech should not be read. At least it should never appear or sound as if you are reading it. An audience is dismayed to see a speaker peering down at a thick sheaf of papers on the lectern, wetting his thumb to turn to the next page.

How to Sound Spontaneous

The best speakers are those who make their words sound spontaneous even if memorized. I've found it's best to learn a speech point by point, not word for word. Careful preparation and a great deal of practicing are required to make it come together smoothly and easily. Mark Twain once said, "It takes three weeks to prepare a good ad-lib speech."

Don't be fooled when you rehearse. It takes longer to deliver a speech than to read it. Most speakers peg along at a hundred words a minute.

"Why should you make a speech? There are four big reasons (left to right): to inspire, to persuade, to entertain, to instruct. I'll tell you how to organize what you say."

Brevity Is an Asset

A sensible plan, if you have been asked to speak to an exact limit, is to talk your speech into a mirror and stop at your allotted time; then cut the speech accordingly. The more familiar you become with your speech, the more confidently you can deliver it.

As anyone who listens to speeches knows, brevity is an asset. Twenty minutes are ideal. An hour is the limit an audience can listen comfortably.

In mentioning brevity, it is worth mentioning that the shortest inaugural address was George Washington's—just 135 words. The longest was William Henry Harrison's in 1841. He delivered a two-hour, nine-thousand-word speech into the teeth of a freezing northeast wind. He came down with a cold the following day, and a month later he died of pneumonia.

Check Your Grammar

Consult a dictionary for proper meanings and pronunciations. Your audience won't know if you're a bad speller, but they will know if you use or pronounce a word improperly. In my first remarks on the dais, I used to thank people for their "fulsome introduction," until I discovered to my dismay that "fulsome" means *offensive* and *insincere.*

On the Podium

It helps one's nerves to pick out three or four people in the audience—preferably in different sectors so that the speaker is apparently giving his attention to the entire room—on whom to focus. Pick out people who seem to be having a good time.

How Questions Help

A question period at the end of a speech is a good notion. One would not ask questions following a tribute to the company treasurer on his retirement, say, but a technical talk or an informative speech can be enlivened with a question period.

The Crowd

The larger the crowd, the easier it is to speak, because the response is multiplied and increased. Most people do not believe this. They peek out from behind the curtain, and if the auditorium is filled to the rafters, they begin to moan softly in the back of their throats.

What About Stage Fright?

Very few speakers escape the so-called "butterflies." There does not seem to be any cure for them, except to realize that they are beneficial rather than harmful, and never fatal. The tension usually means that the speaker, being keyed up, will do a better

"What am I doing wrong? Taking refuge behind the lectern, looking scared to death, shuffling pages and reading my speech. Relax. Come out in the open, gesture, *talk* to your audience."

job. Edward R. Murrow called stage fright "the sweat of perfection." Mark Twain once comforted a fright-frozen friend about to speak: "Just remember they don't expect much." My own feeling is that with thought, preparation and faith in your ideas, you can go out there and expect a pleasant surprise.

And what a sensation it is—to hear applause. Invariably after it dies away, the speaker searches out the program chairman—just to make it known that he's available for next month's meeting.

We asked James Dickey, poet-in-residence at the University of South Carolina, winner of the National Book Award for his collection of poems *Buckdancer's Choice* and author of the novel *Deliverance,* to tell you how to approach poetry so it can bring special pleasure and understanding to your life.

10

How to Enjoy Poetry

by James Dickey

What is poetry? And why has it been around so long? Many have suspected that it was invented as a school subject, because you have to take exams on it. But that is not what poetry is or why it is still around. That's not what it feels like, either. When you really feel it, a new part of you happens, or an old part is renewed, with surprise and delight at being what it is.

Where Poetry Is Coming From

From the beginning, men have known that words and things, words and actions, words and feelings, go together, and that they can go together in thousands of different ways, according to who is using them. Some ways go shallow, and some go deep.

Your Connection with Other Imaginations

The first thing to understand about poetry is that it comes to you from outside you, in books or in words, but that for it to live, something from within you must come to it and meet it and complete it. Your response with your own mind and body and memory and emotions gives the poem its ability to work its magic; if you give to it, it will give to you, and give plenty.

When you read, don't let the poet write down to you; read up to him. Reach for him from your gut out, and the heart and muscles will come into it, too.

Which Sun? Whose Stars?

The sun is new every day, the ancient philosopher Heraclitus said. The sun of poetry is new every day, too, because it is seen in different ways by different people who have lived under it, lived with it, responded to it. Their lives are different from yours, but by means of the special spell that poetry brings to the *fact* of the sun—everybody's sun; yours, too—you can come into possession of many suns: as many as men and women have ever been able to imagine. Poetry makes possible the deepest kind of personal possession of the world.

The most beautiful constellation in the winter sky is Orion, which ancient poets thought looked like a hunter, up there, moving across heaven with his dog Sirius. What is this hunter made out of stars hunting for? What does he mean? Who owns him, if anybody? The poet Aldous Huxley felt that he did, and so, in Aldous Huxley's universe of personal emotion, he did.

> *Up from among the emblems of the*
> *wind into its heart of power,*
> *The Huntsman climbs, and all his*
> *living stars*
> *Are bright, and all are mine.*

Where to Start

The beginning of your true encounter with poetry should be simple. It should bypass all classrooms, all textbooks, courses, examinations and libraries and go straight to the things that make your own existence exist: to your body and nerves and blood and muscles. Find your own way—a secret way that just maybe you don't know yet—to open yourself as wide as you can and as deep as you can to the moment, the *now* of your own existence and the endless mystery of it, and perhaps at the same time to one other thing that is not you, but is out there: a handful of gravel is a good place to start. So is an ice cube—what more mysterious and beautiful *interior* of something has there ever been?

As for me, I like the sun, the source of all living things, and on certain days very good-feeling, too. "Start with the sun," D. H. Lawrence said, "and everything will slowly, slowly happen." Good advice. And a lot *will* happen.

What is more fascinating than a rock, if you really feel it and *look* at it, or more interesting than a leaf?

> *Horses, I mean; butterflies, whales;*
> *Mosses, and stars; and gravelly*
> *Rivers, and fruit.*
> *Oceans, I mean; black valleys; corn;*
> *Brambles, and cliffs; rock, dirt, dust, ice . . .*

Go back and read this list—it is quite a list, Mark Van Doren's list!—item by item. Slowly. Let each of these things call up an image out of your own life.

Think and feel. What moss do you see? Which horse? What field of corn? What brambles are your brambles? Which river is most yours?

The Poem's Way of Going

Part of the spell of poetry is in the rhythm of language, used by poets who understand how powerful a factor rhythm can be, how compelling and unforgettable. Almost anything put into rhyme is more memorable than the same thing said in prose. Why this is, no one knows completely, though the answer is surely rooted far down in the biology by means of which we exist; in the circulation of the blood that goes forth from the heart and comes back, and in the repetition of breathing. Croesus was a rich Greek king, back in the sixth century before Christ, but this tombstone was not his:

No Croesus lies in the grave you see;
I was a poor laborer, and this suits me.

That is plainspoken and definitive. You believe it, and the rhyme helps you believe it and keep it.

Some Things You'll Find Out

Writing poetry is a lot like a contest with yourself, and if you like sports and games and competitions of all kinds, you might like to try writing some. Why not?

The possibilities of rhyme are great. Some of the best fun is in making up your own limericks. There's no reason you can't invent limericks about anything that comes to your mind. No reason. Try it.

The problem is to find three words that rhyme and fit into a meaning. "There was a young man from . . ." *Where* was he from? What situation was he in? How can these things fit into the limerick form—a form everybody knows—so that the rhymes "pay off," and give that sense of completion and inevitability that is so deliciously memorable that nothing else is like it?

How It Goes with You

The more your encounter with poetry deepens, the more your experience of your own life will deepen, and you will begin to see things by means of words, and words by means of things.

You will come to understand the world as it interacts with words, as it can be re-created by words, by rhythms and by images.

You'll understand that this condition is one charged with vital possibilities. You will pick up meaning more quickly—and you will *create* meaning, too, for yourself and for others.

Connections between things will exist for you in ways that they never did before. They will shine with unexpectedness, wide-openness, and you will go toward them, on your own path. "Then," as Dante says, "will your feet be filled with good desire." You will know this is happening the first time you say, of something you never would have noticed before, "Well, would you look at *that!* Who'd 'a thunk it?" (Pause, full of new light.)

"*I* thunk it!"

James Dickey

We asked John Irving, author of *The World According to Garp, The Hotel New Hampshire* and *Setting Free the Bears,* among other novels—and once a hopelessly bad speller himself—to teach you how to improve your spelling.

11

How to Spell

by *John Irving*

Let's begin with the bad news.

If you're a bad speller, you probably think you always will be. There are exceptions to every spelling rule, and the rules themselves are easy to forget. George Bernard Shaw demonstrated how ridiculous spelling rules are. By following the rules, he said, we could spell "fish" this way: *ghoti.* The "f" as it sounds in enou*gh*, the "i" as it sounds in w*o*men, and the "sh" as it sounds in fic*ti*on.

With such rules to follow, no one should feel stupid for being a bad speller. But there are ways to improve. Start by acknowledging the mess that English spelling is in—but have sympathy: English spelling changed with foreign influences. Chaucer wrote "gesse," but "guess," imported earlier by the Norman invaders, finally replaced it. Most early printers in England came from Holland; they brought "ghost" and "gherkin" with them.

If you'd like to intimidate yourself—and remain a bad speller forever—just try to remember the thirteen different ways the sound "sh" can be written:

_sh_oe	suspi_ci_on
_s_ugar	nau_se_ous
o_ce_an	con_sc_ious
i_ss_ue	_ch_aperone
na_ti_on	man_si_on
_sch_ist	fu_chs_ia
_psh_aw	

Now the Good News

The good news is that 90 percent of all writing consists of one thousand basic words. There is, also, a method to most English spelling and a great number of how-to-spell books. Remarkably, all these books propose learning the same rules! Not surprisingly, most of these books are humorless.

Just keep this in mind: If you're familiar with the words you use, you'll probably spell them correctly—and you shouldn't be writing words you're unfamiliar with anyway. *Use* a word—out loud, and more than once—before you try writing it, and make sure (with a new word) that you know what it means before you use it. This means you'll have to look it up in a dictionary, where you'll not only learn what it means, but you'll see how it's spelled. Choose a dictionary you enjoy browsing in, and guard it as you would a diary. You wouldn't lend a diary, would you?

A Tip on Looking It Up

Beside every word I look up in my dictionary, I make a mark. Beside every word I look up more than once, I write a note to myself—about *why* I looked it up. I have looked up "strictly" fourteen times since 1964. I prefer to spell it with a _k_—as in "stric_k_tly." I have looked up "ubiquitous" a dozen times. I can't remember what it means.

Another good way to use your dictionary: When you have to look up a word, for any reason, learn—and learn to *spell*—a *new*

"Love your dictionary."

word at the same time. It can be any useful word on the same page as the word you looked up. Put the date beside this new word and see how quickly, or in what way, you forget it. Eventually, you'll learn it.

Almost as important as knowing what a word means (in order to spell it) is knowing how it's pronounced. It's gov*ern*ment, not gov*er*ment. It's Fe*bru*ary, not Fe*bu*ary. And if you know that *anti*- means against, you should know how to spell *anti*dote and *anti*biotic and *anti*freeze. If you know that *ante*- means before, you shouldn't have trouble spelling *ante*chamber or *ante*cedent.

Some Rules, Exceptions, and Two Tricks

I don't have room to touch on *all* the rules here. It would take a book to do that. But I can share a few that help me most:

What about -*ary* or -*ery*? When a word has a primary accent on the first syllable and a secondary accent on the next-to-last syllable (sec′ re tar′ y), it usually ends in -*ary*. Only six important words with a secondary accent on the next-to-last syllable end in -*ery*:

cemetery	confectionery
millinery	stationery
distillery	(as in pap*e*r)
monastery	

Here's another easy rule. Only four words end in -*efy*. Most people misspell them—with -*ify*, which is usually correct. Just memorize these too, and use -*ify* for all the rest.

stupefy	putrefy
liquefy	rarefy

As a former bad speller, I have learned a few valuable tricks. Any good how-to-spell book will teach you more than these two, but these two are my favorites. Of the eight hundred thousand words in the English language, the most frequently misspelled is alright; just remember that alright is all wrong. You wouldn't write alwrong, would you? That's how you know you should write all right.

The other trick is for the truly *worst* spellers. I mean those of you who spell so badly that you can't get close enough to the right way to spell a word in order to even *find* it in the dictionary. The word you're looking for is there, of course, but you won't find it the way you're trying to spell it. What to do is look up a synonym—another word that means the same thing. Chances are good that you'll find the word you're looking for under the definition of the synonym.

Demon Words and Bugbears

Everyone has a few demon words—they never look right, even when they're spelled correctly. Three of my demons are medi-

"This is one of the longest English words in common use. But don't let the length of a word frighten you. There's a rule for how to spell this one, and you can learn it."

eval, ecstasy and rhythm. I have learned to hate these words, but I have not learned to spell them; I have to look them up every time.

And everyone has a spelling rule that's a bugbear—it's either too difficult to learn or it's impossible to remember. My personal bugbear among the rules is the one governing whether you add -*able* or -*ible.* I can teach it to you, but I can't remember it myself.

You add -*able* to a full word: adapt, adaptable; work, workable. You add -*able* to words that end in *e*—just remember to drop the final *e:* love, lovable. But if the word ends in two *e*'s, like agree, you keep them both: agreeable.

You add -*ible* if the base is not a full word that can stand on its own: credible, tangible, horrible, terrible. You add -*ible* if the root word ends in -*ns:* responsible. You add -*ible* if the root word ends in -*miss:* permissible. You add -*ible* if the root word ends in a soft *c* (but remember to drop the final *e!*): force, forcible.

Got that? I don't have it, and I was introduced to that rule in prep school; with that rule, I still learn one word at a time.

Poor President Jackson

You must remember that it is permissible for spelling to drive you crazy. Spelling had this effect on Andrew Jackson, who once blew his stack while trying to write a Presidential paper. "It's a damn poor mind that can think of only one way to spell a word!" the President cried.

When you have trouble, think of poor Andrew Jackson and know that you're not alone.

What's Really Important

And remember what's really important about good writing is not good spelling. If you spell badly but write well, you should hold your head up. As the poet T. S. Eliot recommended, "Write for as large and miscellaneous an audience as possible"—and don't be overly concerned if you can't spell "miscellaneous." Also remember that you can spell correctly and write well and still be misunderstood. Hold your head up about that, too. As good old G. C. Lichtenberg said, "A book is a mirror: if an ass peers into it, you can't expect an apostle to look out"—whether you spell "apostle" correctly or not.

John Irving

We asked Erma Bombeck, nationally syndicated columnist and author of *Motherhood: The Second Oldest Profession* and other perceptive books about family life, to tell you how to make your child an eager, lifelong reader.

12

How to Encourage Your Child to Read

by Erma Bombeck

When you think about it, most of us were read to sleep. The faster we nodded off . . . the better the book.

We didn't know how good books could be until we grew up and started to read ourselves.

Well, most of us did.

One out of every five American adults is still being read to. They are functionally illiterate. According to the U.S. Department of Education, there are twenty-three million people who can't read a help-wanted ad, the directions on a medication bottle, a menu in a restaurant—or this article. Many who have graduated from high school and college can't do much better.

So, how do you get your kids to read?

If you've read this far, you're halfway home. It means you, as a parent, like to read and want the same enjoyment and skills for your children.

When to Start?

And the sooner you get started the better. In our culture, you have to be able to read to get an education. The education starts sooner than you think. Scientists say that a child has acquired 50 percent of the intelligence she'll eventually have by the time she's only four. She adds another 30 percent by the time she's eight. Between the ages of eight and eighty, there's less brain growth than from seven to eight. (As in the rest of this article, when I mention she or her, I also mean he or him.)

You're lucky. You have the child at home all to yourself during her most dynamic development years—the so-called "peak learning years" when she is literally bursting to grow, stretch, learn and do.

Any reading experience you can give your child before she starts to school will make her a better reader.

Experts have discovered a couple of common threads among children who read well.

One was that their parents provided them with things to read and to write with, such as books, pencils and paper, just to get comfortable with them.

The other thread they share is that their parents read aloud to them. Some parents started the day their babies were born.

I know newborns can't even see a book, but *something* happens when a parent reads aloud. The partnership begins. It doesn't matter what you read the first few months as long as she can hear your voice and feel your warmth.

I once read a steam iron warranty out loud. I was enlightened; the kid figured it was another fairy tale.

Time for Mother Goose

At around six months, pick up *Mother Goose.* Nursery rhymes all have wonderfully pleasing and playful word combinations to delight her. And when she's able to see well, make sure your book has pictures with large, colorful, easy-to-grasp illustrations for her to wonder about.

Working mothers in the home and those who have a second job deserve a few minutes of quiet time to relax and share a story with their child away from the noise and interruptions.

When you move on to storybooks and children's novels, be sure they're right for both of you. C. S. Lewis, author of *The Chronicles of Narnia,* said, "A book which is enjoyed only by children is a bad children's book."

Three-year-olds love "The Three Little Pigs," "Little Red Riding Hood" and "The Gingerbread Man." Stories like these tell a child that if you do what's right and are brave and smart about it, you'll come through.

But wait a year before you try more sophisticated fairy tales like "Snow White" and "Rapunzel," with their evil-minded people—a concept a tiny child isn't emotionally prepared to grapple with yet.

Go Ahead—Ham It Up

When you're reading out loud, ham it up. Use inflections. You want to awaken her interest in reading, not put her to sleep. And if you see your child getting tired, try to end on a cliffhanger to get her back for more tomorrow.

Four-year-olds are ready to be introduced to the beginning classics, such as the stories of the Brothers Grimm and Hans Christian Andersen. By that age they can take wicked queens in their stride. (If they've watched the national average of six thousand hours of television before they start school, a wicked queen could be a heroine.)

As you read to your child, don't be surprised when she starts to pick out letters and even words. She's making those connections between the sounds and the symbols on the page. Now it's time to get an ABC book and start to familiarize her with the alphabet. A good abecedarius is *A Peaceable Kingdom* by Alice and Martin Provensen.

The producers of "Sesame Street" found that kids who know their ABC's get into reading far more readily than the kids who don't.

As your child picks up certain words, help her sound them

"This is one good way to make the connection between words and what they stand for: Label the things often used in her room."

out syllable by syllable and understand their meaning. Later, ease her into phrases and sentences.

A word of caution: Don't push. She'll tell you when she's ready. Go at her pace and keep her excited about the *idea* of reading.

"What! Teach My Own Child to Read?"

Most of us who aren't teachers are apprehensive about doing anything that might jeopardize the teaching process. Don't worry. Many educators say we can't do any harm, and it is far better to teach her at the time she's ready. So go to it. Besides, one-on-one teaching is the best kind. I love Dr. Seuss, who said, "You really can't teach reading as a science. Love gets mixed up in it."

Other ways to help:

Encourage her to speak up. Good oral skills make good readers.

Open up her world. Give her something to talk about such as a trip to the zoo, a concert, or a bus ride.

Label things in her room, like "Bed," "Truck," "Doll," so that she can make the association.

Read street signs and names on packages in the supermarket.

As soon as she can write her name, get her a library card. And don't forget a trip to the local bookstore, where she can pick out and keep her very own book to go back to time and again.

And make the most of "reality reading." Even junk mail can be of value here. She'll love to open it and it might encourage her to write a letter.

Leave handwritten notes for her on the refrigerator. Check road maps before a trip.

When all the Bombecks went on vacation, we took turns reading from a book telling us where we were going and what points of interest to look for. It not only made better readers out of the kids, it kept them from killing one another.

Newspapers are great incentives. She can read the weather map, TV listings, not to mention the comics.

Pick the Right Books for Her Age

Keep stoking the fire. First- and second-graders like jokes, riddles and humor, plus monsters, mysteries and animals.

Third- and fourth-graders like the same things a little more advanced. They're ready for magazines, dictionaries and other reference books.

Fifth- and sixth-grade boys go for sports and mysteries, but at this age girls are starting to get into romantic novels.

What to do about her reading things you don't approve of— "trashy" books, comic books and the like? In my book, any book they read themselves is a good book. Even *Spider-Man** can eventually catch you in the web of *War and Peace.*

If your child doesn't respond to reading as early as you hope, don't be discouraged. Some are ready sooner than others.

* SPIDER-MAN℗ Marvel Comics Group

"In my book, any book is a good book.
Even *Spider-Man* can eventually catch you
in the web of *War and Peace.*"

If your child has *serious* trouble with reading, in any grade, there
are steps you can take, including remedial classes and reading
clinics. Check your school for further help and information.

Start an Adventure

I cannot begin to tell you what the love of reading will do for
your children. It will open doors of curiosity. It will titillate their
desire to see places they thought were make-believe. It softens
loneliness, fills the gaps of boredom, creates role models and
changes the course of their very lives.

My children started out reading designer labels. It certainly changed my life.

Erma Bombeck

We asked Russell Baker, winner of the Pulitzer Prize for his book *Growing Up* and for his essays in The New York *Times* (the latest collection in book form is called *The Rescue of Miss Yaskell and Other Pipe Dreams*), to help you make better use of punctuation, one of the printed word's most valuable tools.

13

How to Punctuate

by Russell Baker

When you write, you make a sound in the reader's head. It can be a dull mumble—that's why so much government prose makes you sleepy—or it can be a joyful noise, a sly whisper, a throb of passion.

Listen to a voice trembling in a haunted room:

"And the silken, sad, uncertain rustling of each purple curtain thrilled me—filled me with fantastic terrors never felt before . . ."

That's Edgar Allan Poe, a master. Few of us can make paper speak as vividly as Poe could, but even beginners will write better once they start listening to the sound their writing makes.

One of the most important tools for making paper speak in your own voice is punctuation. "Punctuation," someone has said, "gives the silent page the breath of life."

When speaking aloud, you punctuate constantly—with body language. Your listener hears commas, dashes, question marks, exclamation points, quotation marks as you shout, whisper, pause, wave your arms, roll your eyes, wrinkle your brow.

In writing, punctuation plays the role of body language. It helps readers hear you the way you want to be heard. Careful use of those little marks emphasizes the sound of your distinctive voice and keeps the reader from becoming bored or confused.

"Gee, Dad, Have I Got to Learn All Them Rules?"

Don't let the rules scare you. For they aren't hard and fast. Think of them as guidelines. Remember: Punctuation is a tool to make your voice sound clearly in the reader's head. It exists to serve *you.* Don't be bullied into serving *it.*

Am I saying, "Go ahead and punctuate as you please"? Absolutely not. Use your own common sense, remembering that you can't expect readers to work to decipher what you're trying to say. Most readers won't.

What's important is that the marks help the reader hear you precisely. I've published several million words, and I've had almost every one read aloud to me, or read it aloud to myself, before sending it to an editor. If it doesn't sound right, I make changes. Often it's a simple matter of changing a punctuation mark.

Have someone else read your material aloud. You'll be surprised how quickly you can *hear* a punctuation mistake and correct it.

Loose System vs. Tight

There are two basic systems of punctuation:

1. The loose or open system, which tries to capture the way body language punctuates when you talk.

2. The tight, closed structural system, which hews closely to the sentence's grammatical structure.

Most writers use a little of both. In any case, we use much less punctuation than two hundred or even fifty years ago. (Glance into Edward Gibbon's *Decline and Fall of the Roman Empire,* first published about two hundred years ago, for an example of the tight structural system at its most elegant.)

Whichever system you prefer, be warned: Punctuation marks cannot save a sentence that is badly put together. If you have to struggle over commas, semicolons and parenthesis marks, you've probably built a sentence that's never going to fly,

"My tools of the trade should be your tools, too. Good use of punctuation can help you build a more solid, more readable sentence."

no matter how you tinker with it. Throw it away and build a new one to a simpler design. The better your sentence, the easier it is to punctuate.

Choosing the Right Tool

There are thirty main punctuation marks, but you'll need fewer than a dozen for most writing.

By using them judiciously, you can raise your voice, pause briefly, stop to look around, sound mystified, lift an eyebrow, interrupt yourself for a wisecrack, imitate someone else's voice, and lots more. I can't show you in this small space how they all work, so I'll stick to the ten most important—and even then I can only hit highlights. For more details, check your dictionary or a good grammar.

Comma [,]

This is the most widely used mark of all. It's also the toughest and most controversial. I've seen aging editors almost come to blows over the comma. If you can handle it without sweating, the others will be easy. Here's my policy:

1. Use a comma after a long introductory phrase or clause:

    After stealing the crown jewels from the Tower of London, I went home for tea.

2. If the introductory material is short, forget the comma:

    After the theft I went home for tea.

3. But use it if the sentence would be confusing without it, like this:

    The day before, I'd robbed the Bank of England.

4. Use a comma to separate elements in a series:

    I robbed the Denver Mint, the Bank of England, the Tower of London and my piggy bank.

Notice there is no comma before "and" in the series. This is common style nowadays, but some book publishers still use a comma there, too.

5. Use a comma to separate independent clauses that are joined by a conjunction like *and, but, for, or, nor, because* or *so:*

    I shall return the crown jewels, for they are too heavy to wear.

6. Use a comma to set off a mildly parenthetical word grouping that isn't essential to the sentence:

    Girls, who have always interested me, usually differ from boys.

Do not use commas if the word grouping *is* essential to the sentence's meaning:

    Girls who interest me know how to tango.

7. Use a comma in direct address:

    Your majesty, please hand over the crown.

8. And between proper names and titles:

    Montague Sneed, Director of Scotland Yard, was assigned to the case.

9. And to separate elements of geographical address:

    Director Sneed comes from Chicago, Illinois, and now lives in London, England.

Generally speaking, use a comma where you'd normally

pause briefly in speech. For a long pause or the completion of a thought, use a period.

If you confuse the comma with the period, you'll get a run-on sentence:

> *The Bank of England is located in London, I rushed right over to rob it.*

Semicolon [;]

A more sophisticated mark than the comma, the semicolon separates two main clauses in a sentence, but it keeps those two thoughts more tightly linked than a period can:

> *I steal crown jewels; she steals hearts.*

Dash [—] and Parentheses [( )]

Warning! Use sparingly. The dash SHOUTS. Parentheses whisper. Shout too often, people stop listening; whisper too much, people become suspicious of you.

The dash creates a dramatic pause to prepare for an expression needing strong emphasis:

> *I'll marry you—if you'll rob Topkapi with me.*

Parentheses help you pause quietly to drop in some chatty information not vital to your story:

> *Despite Betty's daring spirit ("I love robbing your piggy bank," she often said), she was a terrible dancer.*

Quotation Marks [" "]

These tell the reader you're reciting the exact words someone said or wrote. Here's the form:

> *Betty said, "I can't tango."*
>
> Or: *"I can't tango," Betty said.*

Notice that the comma comes before the quote marks in the

first example, but comes inside them in the second. Not logical? Never mind. Do it that way anyhow.

Sometimes punctuating with quote marks can look silly. Here's an example for advanced students to ponder:

Did you ask Betty, "Is this what you call a tango?"?

Colon [:]

A colon is a tip-off to get ready for what's next: a list, or tables, a long quotation or an explanation. This article is riddled with colons. Too many, maybe, but the message is: "Stay on your toes; it's coming at you."

Apostrophe [']

The big headache is with possessive nouns. If the noun is singular add *'s:*

I hated Betty's tango.

If the noun is plural, simply add an apostrophe after the *s:*

Those are the girls' coats.

The same applies for singular nouns ending in *s,* like Dickens:

This is Dickens's best book.

And in plural:

This is the Dickenses' cottage.

The possessive pronouns *hers* and *its* have no apostrophe. If you write *it's,* you are saying *it is.*

Keep Cool

You know about ending a sentence with a period [.] or a question mark [?]. Do it. Sure, you can also end with an exclamation mark [!], but must you? Usually, it just makes you sound breathless and silly. Make your writing generate its own excitement. Filling

"Punctuation puts body language on the printed page. Show bewilderment with a question mark, a whisper with parentheses, emphasis with an exclamation point."

the paper with !!!! won't make up for what your writing has failed to do.

Too many exclamation marks make me think the writer is talking about the panic in his own head.

Don't sound panicky. End with a period. I am serious. A period. Understand?

Well . . . sometimes a question mark is okay.

Russell Baker

Bibliography

Benét, William Rose. *The Reader's Encyclopedia.* New York: Thomas Y. Crowell Co., 1965

Fadiman, Clifton. *The Lifetime Reading Plan.* New York: Thomas Y. Crowell Co., 1978.

———. *Reading I've Liked.* New York: Simon & Schuster, 1958.

Fiedler, Leslie. *Love and Death in the American Novel.* New York: Stein & Day, 1975.

Gardner, John. *On Moral Fiction.* New York: Basic Books, 1978.

Kronenberger, Louis. *Novelists on Novelists.* Garden City, N.Y.: Anchor Books, 1962.

Nabokov, Vladimir. *Lectures on Literature.* New York: Harcourt, Brace, Jovanovich, 1980.

———. *Lectures on Russian Literature.* New York: Harcourt, Brace, Jovanovich, 1981.

Powys, John Cowper. *Enjoyment of Literature.* New York: Simon & Schuster, 1938.

Priestley, J. B. *Literature and Western Man.* New York: Harper & Brothers, 1960.

Scott-James, R. A. *The Making of Literature.* Folcroft, Pa.: Folcroft Library Editions, 1973.

Seymour-Smith, Martin. *Novels and Novelists.* New York: St. Martin's Press, 1980.

Weber, J. Sherwood. *Good Reading.* New York: New American Library, 1980.

NOTE: *The Viking Portable Series* offers compact and provocative collections of vital writings by classic authors, with readable and interesting in-depth introductions to help make what you read even more enjoyable. Try them.

How to Read an Annual Report

Costales, S. B. *The Guide to Understanding Financial Statements.* New York: McGraw-Hill Book Co., 1979.

Graham, Benjamin, and Charles McGolrick. *The Interpretation of Financial Statements.* New York: Harper & Row Publishers, 1978.

Tracy, John A. *How to Read a Financial Report.* New York: John Wiley & Sons, 1980.

Understanding Financial Statements. Booklet, Bank of America, 1980.

Understanding Financial Statements. Booklet, New York Stock Exchange, 1978.

How to Make a Speech
Adler, Mortimer J. *How to Speak, How to Listen.* New York: Macmillan, 1983.
Braude, Jacob M. *The Complete Art of Public Speaking.* New York: Bantam Books, 1970.
Sarnoff, Dorothy. *Speech Can Change Your Life.* New York: Dell Publishing Co., 1970.

How to Enjoy Poetry
Auden, W. H. *The Dyer's Hand.* New York: Random House, 1962.
Ciardi, John, and Miller Williams. *How Does a Poem Mean?* Boston: Houghton Mifflin Co., 1975.
Koch, Kenneth, and Kate Farrell. *Sleeping on the Wing.* New York: Random House, 1981.
Trilling, Lionel. *Prefaces to the Experience of Literature.* New York: Harcourt Brace Jovanovich, 1979.

How to Encourage Your Child to Read
Bettelheim, Bruno, and Karen Zelan. *On Learning to Read.* New York: Alfred A. Knopf, 1982.
Butler, Dorothy. *Babies Need Books.* New York: Atheneum Publishers, 1982.
Kimmel, Margaret Mary, and Elizabeth Segal. *For Reading Out Loud.* New York: Delacorte Press, 1983.
Kusnetz, Len. *Your Child Can Be a Super Reader.* Roslyn, N.Y.: Learning House Publishers, 1980.
Lee, Barbara, and Masha K. Rudman. *Leading to Reading.* New York: Berkley Publishing Corp., 1982.
Trelease, Jim. *The Read-Aloud Handbook.* New York: Penguin Books, 1982.

How to Punctuate
The Associated Press Stylebook and Libel Manual. Reading, Mass.: Addison-Wesley Publishing Co., 1982.
The Chicago Manual of Style. 13th rev. ed. Chicago and London: University of Chicago Press, 1982.
Editors of *Reader's Digest. Success with Words.* Pleasantville, N.Y.: Reader's Digest Assn., 1983.
Follett, Wilson. *Modern American Usage.* New York: Hill & Wang, 1966.
Gordon, Karen Elizabeth. *The Well-Tempered Sentence.* New York: Ticknor & Fields, 1983.

Hodges, John C., and Mary E. Whitten. *Harbrace College Handbook.* 9th ed. New York: Harcourt Brace Jovanovich, 1982.

The New York Times Manual of Style and Usage. New York: Quadrangle/ The New York Times Book Co., 1976.

You will find concise punctuation guides in the back of many good comprehensive dictionaries. Always make sure you keep a well-thumbed one beside your elbow. Two good examples:

Webster's New World Dictionary of the American Language. 2nd college ed. New York: Simon & Schuster, 1983.

The American Heritage Dictionary. Boston: Houghton Mifflin Company, 1982.

VITALLY IMPORTANT NOTE:

There is a short, short book that is easy to read. You should read it several times, then keep it close by wherever you sit down to write. If you've read all the articles in the book you now have in hand, you'll have found that many of our experts recommend it:

The Elements of Style by William Strunk, Jr., and E. B. White. 3rd ed. New York: Macmillan Publishing Co., 1979.